# build like a pro

# table of contents

DESIGN & PLANNING

# CONTRACTORS & BIDDING

## THE CONSTRUCTION CONTRACT

# THE JOBSITE

# ABOUT THE AUTHOR

Matt Deal has built over 1,500 houses, townhomes and condominiums in a career spanning forty years as a general building contractor, homebuilder and residential developer. He is also a talented residential designer having designed over one hundred individual houses, a number of commercial buildings and several condominium and townhome projects.

Matt began working in construction in 1971 as a carpenter's apprentice in Salem, Oregon. The following year he moved to Hawaii where he worked with tools as a framing carpenter on resort developments and private homes. He also poured concrete, hung drywall, applied stucco and generally performed just about every task needed to build a custom house.

By 1974 he had earned his general contractors' licenses in California and Hawaii.

In the mid-seventies he designed his first home, built it on spec with two buddies, and sold it for a profit. From that start he began designing and building custom homes for clients on the Island of Kauai, eventually completing over two dozen design/build projects.

By the mid-1980s Matt had started working in commercial construction, bidding and building projects in both the public and private sectors including the Lihue Civic Center on Kauai. In 1995 he moved to Colorado where he started Parkside Homes, eventually building over 1,300 new homes worth over a quarter billion dollars. He developed all the contract documents, management systems and quality control protocols needed to successfully build up to 150 houses a year. In this book he shares that experience with you.

During the course of his career Matt has collaborated with architects, navigated building departments, prepared several thousand construction documents, and managed hundreds of sub-contractors and construction workers. In this book his experience shows through on nearly every page with insights and streetwise tips you won't find anywhere else.

Today Matt lives in Encinitas, California, where he continues to work in residential building as a general contractor and owner's representative. His website is www.encore-builders.com.

# introduction

# WHAT THIS BOOK IS ABOUT

If you are planning a home renovation or building a new custom home from the ground up, this book contains valuable advice and insights which you simply cannot do without. While there are lots of books written about "how" to build a house or remodel a kitchen, there is a lack of books about how to "manage" a project. This book addresses how to request, assess and purchase building, design and construction consulting services.

This book is not going to tell you how to save "thousands"; nor will I promise that you can manage a complex project "part time". You most likely won't; and you can't.

3

You might think you can do it better than a qualified and experienced contractor. Perhaps you can; but please read this book first. You might reconsider the risks involved in managing your own project. Before undertaking any construction project, large or small, you need adequate preparation and understanding of the challenges involved. There are many pitfalls awaiting the unwary; my goal is to guide you through and past them.

Whether you elect to be your own contractor, or to hire professionals to do the job for you, the lessons and information in this book will make for a more successful project, keep your stress level down and, hopefully, keep your marriage alive and well.

I have intentionally left a large margin at the top of each page so that you may makes notes. This book is intended to be used, marked up and gotten dirty.

| What This Book Is About | What This Book Is NOT About |
| --- | --- |
| How to inform yourself | How to design your home or kitchen |
| The process of managing a project | How to get financing |
| Tools to manage the process | How to buy a lot |
| How to make good decisions | Framing, plumbing or roofing |
| Critical management tools | What materials to use |
| Mistakes to avoid | How to "save" money |

4

This book is going to share with you how an experienced contractor approaches a building project and how he manages for success and profit. The lessons learned will expedite the process, illuminate uncertainty, reduce stress and should, in the end, save both time and money. Happy building!

# THE DREAM

Figure 1:  The Great Pyramids

No, we're not going to build pyramids in this book; but a good foundation is important to every construction project, both literally and figuratively.  Civilizations are documented by their intellectual record, but also, more visually, by their buildings.  Everyone knows of the ancient Romans and Egyptians.  There were other ancient civilizations, but most of us know little about them.  What sets the Romans and Egyptians apart from the others in our consciousness?  Simply, it is their buildings – the Coliseum in Rome; the pyramids along the Nile.  They loved to build...and so do we.

Now that you have decided to remodel your kitchen, add a room, or maybe even build your dream house, you are about to become a part of that tradition.  You've spent time flipping through home magazines and clipping ideas; and spent hours watching HGTV.  You're ready to go.  Or are you?

Just where do you start?  What comes first?  Oh my, this suddenly is way more complicated than I thought.  Even more intimidating:  everyone in the process – the architects, the builders, the workers – knows more about building than you do.

Don't worry; we're here to help.  A building project is managed the same way a building is built – by starting at the bottom, one brick at a time, and putting all the pieces together into a harmonious whole.

Many of the topics in this book apply to new construction – a custom home, for instance.  Although much of the planning section may not apply to a kitchen remodel, for instance, other sections of the book have universal application.

# WARNING:  CONSTRUCTION IS MESSY

You need to understand what you are getting into.  Construction is, in many ways, organized chaos.  And Mr. Murphy, of the famous Law, shows up on every job – without exception.  If it can go wrong, it will go wrong.

Figure 2:  Never let your project become this messy.

Construction is messy, it's dirty, it's disruptive and it's confusing.  The workers are an independent minded bunch, and the contractors can be too. Architects can be prima donnas.   But the end results can bring lasting satisfaction and joy to your life. You need to understand that there will be challenges along the way, and prepare for them.  The bigger the project, the bigger the challenges.

Your best defense against disruption, chaos and mess is knowledge.   It is not necessary to know how to install a sink or to frame a wall.  I've built over 1,300 houses and I know very little about electrical wiring, for instance; but I do know how to manage the "process" of building.  I know how to ask the right questions, and when; I am able to be in control of every project I undertake, even if it is new and different from what I have done before, because I have the base knowledge that comes from experience. I am going to share that knowledge with you and, hopefully, after reading this book, you will have the confidence you need to bravely undertake your project.

If you have confidence in your ability to stay in control, you will stay in control. This book is written to give you the tools to be in control. It is about how the building process works. When you understand how the process works, you can make it work for you. Together we will make your project easier, more manageable and more successful than you ever thought possible. You will be in charge, and stay in charge.

# THE FOUR PHASES OF EVERY BUILDING PROJECT

To bring order out of chaos, in this book I have tried to follow the project process sequentially, although this is not always strictly possible. There are often several activities or processes overlapping or unfolding in parallel as your project takes shape.

> "If you don't know where you are going, you'll end up someplace else."
>
> — Yogi Berra

9

There are four basic phases in every project:

## FEASIBILITY · PLANNING · PRE-CONSTRUCTION · CONSTRUCTION

Each phase has a greater or lesser number of activities associated with it. Many of them overlap – such as design and cost of construction – where the decisions or results of the one affect the other

.

## Feasibility

Feasibility addresses the fundamental question: is my project doable? Without determining whether you can actually do what you think you want to do, there is no point in planning to do it. Sounds simple, but all too often homeowners get caught up in the excitement of planning a project only to discover zoning or other roadblocks they had realized existed; or failed to realistically prepare financially for the costs involved.

## Planning

Planning discusses the steps in actually designing your project, and how to manage that portion of the process. It includes a discussion of how plans are organized, how to engage planning and design professionals, and the different choices you have. Design choices and how to design your house or project is not part of this book, but is left to the many books written on the subject. How to make choices is part of this book, and our goal is to give you the information you need to make good choices.

## Pre-Construction

Pre-construction leads the reader through getting ready to build. Although the plans may be complete, there's lots to do before you actually start pushing dirt. We discuss choosing a contractor, bidding, contract documents, insurance, and other topics critical to managing the work. We discuss how to stay out of trouble; and how to get out of trouble if you are unfortunate enough to get into trouble.

## Construction

Construction is the part we've all been waiting for; it's when all the planning and preparation turns into action – something you can see and touch. It's fun and it's exciting – if you've prepared well. We show you how to keep control and to bring the project in on time, on budget and with the quality you want and expect.

For each phase we give you tools to assess your needs and discuss the resources available to you. We help you sort through those resources by discussing when a resource is appropriate, or when another choice might make more sense. Throughout we have tried to apply our experience for your benefit to create a useful guide as you contemplate or undertake your own construction project.

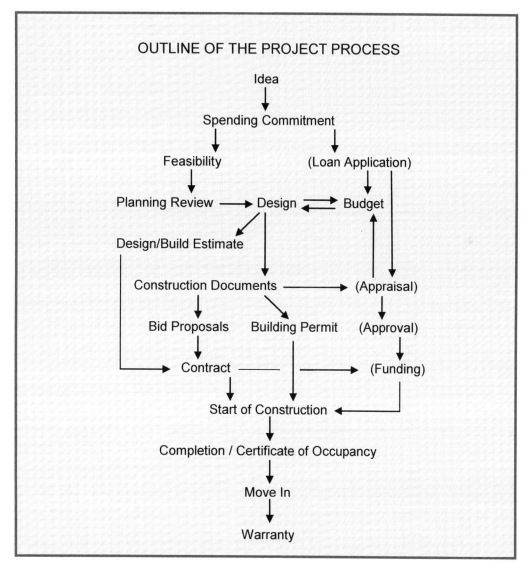

Figure 3: This chart follows a typical construction project from beginning to end.

feasibility

# WHAT COMES FIRST

The first step in the process is to determine the feasibility of your project. It makes no sense to spend time and money preparing a beautiful set of plans only to then find out the project is not doable.

A project may not be buildable for any number of reasons. Chief among these are zoning restrictions, but other reasons may include lack of utility services, unstable soils, financial constraints, community opposition or homeowner association rules.

This section will introduce the concept of the General Plan and the Zoning Code, when they apply to your project, how to deal with them when they do, and who can help you. We also look at the difference between the planning department and the building department.

15

## Big Project or Little Project?

Big projects involve more than little projects. Although the information in this book is useful if you are managing any project, much of what this book is about relates to bigger projects.

**Examples of Big Projects**

New house from the ground up

Room addition

Redesign and rebuild kitchen

Whole house renovation

Any project requiring design or zoning review

**Examples of Little Projects**

Redo shower or guest bathroom

Redo kitchen cabinets and tops

Add a trellis in the back yard*

16

* Be careful; if it is outside, even the seemingly smallest project can become a big project if planning or design review is required. Also, assume the neighbors are watching, and do NOT assume they are as enthusiastic about your project as you are. Many, if not most, permit complaints are turned in by neighbors.

## Spending Commitment

First, determine your budget, or, more accurately, your spending commitment. How much are you willing to spend? Be realistic; without sufficient funds your project cannot get built, and you don't want to run out of money mid-project. At this early stage you will not have an exact budget, or even a preliminary budget – but you don't need one. All you need to establish is your ballpark comfort zone for spending money. Once your comfort level is established, then the scope of your project can be defined.

feasibility

> "We didn't actually overspend our budget. The allocation simply fell short of our expenditure"
>
> — Keith Davis

Still, I know you want some help. A good resource is Remodeling Magazine's annual cost/value survey. The link to the 2013 survey is http://www.remodeling.hw.net/2013/costvsvalue/national.aspx.

Following are a few examples of remodeling project costs (national averages):

17

| COST OF SELECTED REMODELING PROJECTS (National Averages) | |
|---|---|
| Kitchen (minor) | $ 18,500 |
| Kitchen (major) | $ 54,000 |
| Bathroom Remodel | $ 15,000 |
| Bathroom Addition | $ 37,500 |
| Basement Finish | $ 61,000 |
| Family Room Addition | $ 79,000 |
| Garage Addition | $ 49,000 |
| Master Suite Addition | $101,000 |
| Second Floor Addition | $150,000 |

# REGULATIONS

## Is It Allowed?

But all the money in the world won't buy approval of a project that fails to comply with the land use rules where you want to build; or that lacks compliance with the building codes. Compliance with building codes is usually pretty straightforward, but determining what is allowed by the land use codes can be challenging, confusing and frustrating. It helps to understand why these rules exist and how they will affect your project.

Every state, county and city in the United States regulates building to one degree or another. The development of buildings and cities is subject to planning regulations and review; the construction of buildings is subject to building codes overseen by building departments and inspectors. The rational for planning is to ensure the orderly development of cities and urban areas, the preservation of rural areas and to enhance the quality of life.

Although some form of building regulation has existed since ancient times[1], modern building codes first began to appear in Europe and the United States in the mid-nineteenth century, and the first zoning codes early in the last century.

Virtually no structure, or improvement to a structure, may be built absent compliance with planning regulations or without a building permit. It is helpful to understand the planning and permitting processes and how they can affect your project.

18

---

[1] References to building regulations are found in the Code of Hammurabi and in the Old Testament.

feasibility

## The General Plan

A general plan is a philosophical document meant to guide the development of a city, town or county. It sets forth goals, guidelines for achieving those goals, and creates a land use map in furtherance of its stated goals. It is the master plan from which all other planning and development activities flow. The zoning code and zoning map are the technical implementation of the general plan. Some states, such as California, mandate on a state level that every city or town create a general plan setting forth development goals and guidelines for the community. General plans are heavy on planning philosophy and often include design "parameters" and rules which may be problematical in practical execution and will generally tend to make you crazy. Nevertheless, they form the basis which guides the zoning code and guides all planning decisions made by the city planners. You can't avoid them; so it's best to know how to work your way through them.

**19**

## The Planning Department

Planning is generally implemented at the county and city level, although some states, such as Hawaii, have state level regulations and authority. There are also federal laws, such as the National Environmental Protection Act (NEPA), which can affect your plans.

Development and building regulation is usually delegated to local jurisdictions – towns and cities; the county in unincorporated areas. (As a note, county regulations are usually much less stringent than towns or cities, except those for those regulations enacted pursuant to federal or state requirements.) In many states there is some level of state involvement.[2] Other states have

---

[2] For instance, the State of Hawaii has two parallel sets of land use rules – the Land Use Commission at the state level, and the zoning codes at the county level (except for Honolulu,

less direct state involvement, principally limited to legislation mandating certain services, percentages of affordable housing, etc., which are enforced by the local jurisdictions. The most well-known and visible of the macro-government building regulations is the Americans with Disabilities Act. Some cities go even further and mandate that all new houses be accessible (or convertible) even if the owner is not handicapped, and in fact does not even want those features included.

Examples zoning districts are residential, commercial or industrial. There are numerous others and almost endless subdivisions and permutations of the basic districts. The execution and enforcement of the general plan and the zoning code falls to the staff of the planning department. Among other duties, the planning department is responsible for assessing traffic impacts and impacts on city services including water and sewer, parks, libraries and other public facilities and services.

If your project triggers any zoning or planning issues you (or your consultant) will come into contact with your local planning department. Your project may be assigned to a particular planner with whom you will work to resolve any planning issues. These issues may seem obscure, pointless or just plain stupid to you, but do not let any frustration boil over into anger or a confrontation with your planner. Your planner can be your friend, or he can be your nemesis. Always be patient and polite; remember, the planner's job is to interpret the zoning code and general plan and apply them to your project while your goal is simply to get the design you want approved – generally without sympathy to any restrictions imposed by the planning code. If you maintain a good relationship, despite all the obstacles (which may often seem relentless), you will have a much better chance of getting all, or at least some, of what you want. If you become confrontational, you will lose any sympathy

20

---

there are no city governments in Hawaii; each island being its own county.) Any development must comply with both sets of land use rules.

your planner may have had and your application will likely find its way to the bottom of the pile.

Often the secret is finding a route through the zoning code – frequently byzantine – to reach the result you want. Finding the loophole, if you will. In particularly tricky situations expert knowledge of the code will be essential. This is where a planning consultant, or "expeditor" can be invaluable to your success or failure. More on expeditors later.

## Zoning

The first zoning code in the United States was enacted by the City of New York in 1916 in response to neighbors' complaints about the shadows cast by the Equitable Life Assurance skyscraper. Since that first code, zoning codes have been enacted in every major U.S. city except Houston, and throughout the world. Zoning establishes geographic "zones" with rules for use – such as residential or commercial – density, setbacks and even design of buildings within those zones. Cities typically create zoning maps delineating the boundaries of the different zones.

First you must determine the zoning designation of your property; then determine whether your proposed project is a permitted use within that zone. What might at first seem a simple answer is often more complex than it first appears. For instance, you might determine that your property is zoned residential and so conclude that your planned bedroom addition is a permitted use. While that may be true, there are usually multiple other factors in play. Among them are lot coverage, floor area ratio and property line set-backs. Sometimes buildings are within historic or other special districts with severe restrictions on how they may be modified.

21

As you are considering your project you need to first determine the zoning issues involved, if any. Most cities and towns publish their zoning codes and maps online, so you can often do your research from your computer at home. For instance, go the city website, find the planning department link and look for the zoning code links. Often you can simply type in "zoning code Denver", for example, in a Google search.

**22**

First open the map and find your property and identify the zone within which it falls. Then go to the zoning code and search for the section which sets forth the rules and standards for your zone. Often there will be usage tables, set-back tables and other specific information. Also look for other applicable information in the general sections of the code and the development standards. For residential uses, there are often multiple sub-categories.

Finally, try to determine if your property is in a special district. Examples of special districts are historic preservation, waterfront, hillside or high fire danger. These special districts are sometimes called overlays and add a level of requirements beyond the basic zone requirements.

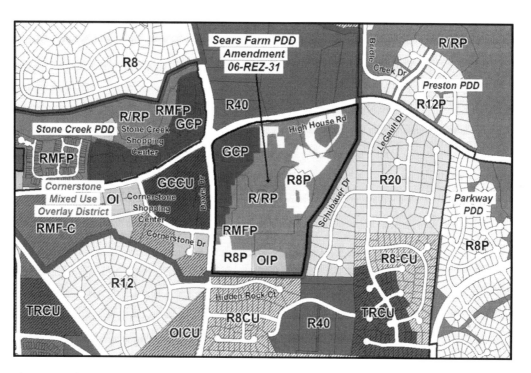

Figure 4: This zoning map is fairly typical, showing residential (R) and commercial (GC) zones. The various zones are color coded.

## Special Zones

Special zones, or overlays, are a parallel universe to the zoning code (which is a parallel universe to the general plan). Special zones identify special, usually physical, conditions which apply to areas of land regardless of their general plan or zoning designation. Following is a brief discussion of several common special zones.

## Flood Zones

You will need to know if your property is in a flood zone. Flood zones are determined by FEMA (the Federal Emergency Management Agency) and delineated on the FIRM (flood insurance rate map), usually simply referred to as the "flood map". The flood map categorizes all land in the United States as being in one of several zones, based upon the likelihood of flooding using standard criteria. The FIRM determines if you will be able to obtain federally guaranteed flood insurance on your home.

Congress authorized the National Flood Insurance Program in 1968, and the first flood maps were published in the early 1970's. Most municipalities will regulate your ability to build in flood zones; however many pre-70's houses were built, and remain, in flood zones. You may find restrictions on what you may do in the way of home construction or remodeling if your property is in a floodway or a flood zone. Flood maps are also subject to revision from time to time.

Although permits to build are usually obtainable in a flood zone, special conditions may be imposed and federal backed flood insurance may not be obtainable. Lacking flood insurance on a home located in a flood zone virtually eliminates the possibility of obtaining a mortgage loan. Generally any building at all is prohibited in a floodway.[3]

For those who desire a thorough understanding of flood maps, FEMA publishes an online tutorial at www.fema.gov/media/fhm/firm/ot_firm.htm.

---

[3] The floodway is the actually course of flowing water in the event of a flood. A flood zone is the area anticipated to be covered by standing water in the event of a flood. Flood zones are classified by frequency and depth. There are also coastal zone areas which predict tsunami impact zones.

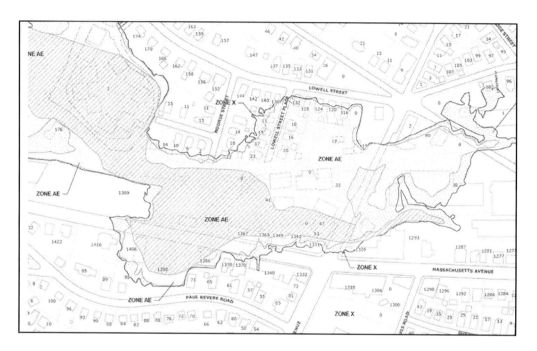

Figure 5: This is an example of a flood insurance rate map (FIRM) showing roads, buildings and flood zones. Flood maps can be found at your local planning department.

## Fire Hazard Zones

Some areas at high risk of wildfires may have special construction requirements which you will need to consider if you are in such an area. Special requirements may include fire sprinklers, fire-proof roofing and siding and combustible-free landscape zones. Many areas in southern California and Texas have fire hazard zones.

## Hillside Zones

Properties on steep slopes are often subject to special considerations, both structurally and visually.

## Coastal

Assume that any property on or near a body of water will be subject to special review. You may find that building heights, architectural design, view planes, colors and other factors will be subject to regulation or negotiation. It oftens seems that your neighbors have as much to say about your property as you do. Ocean coastal areas are especially fraught with challenges for the homeowner and utilizing the assistance of an expert is usually good advice (see "Expeditors" below).

## Historical Districts

Historical Districts can be more fraught with emotion than even coastal zones. You may find that you are unable to make even basic changes to a building designated as a historical building, or included in a historical district – even down to being unable to replace old windows with modern, energy efficient windows[4]. You may find that any change you make is being designed by a committee of your neighbors or special board volunteers. Be prepared for hours of negotiation and a great deal of frustration.

If this all sounds too daunting, take a trip down to the planning department. Most departments have a counter service where a staff planner is on duty who will help you get the answers to your questions. A simple word of advice, however – do as much homework as you can before you visit the

---

[4] Despite official policy encouraging the replacement of old windows.

counter. The planner will appreciate it and the more clearly you can ask your questions, the better the quality of the information you will receive.

---

**DO I NEED HELP?**

Big Project – yes, usually recommended          Small Project – probably not

---

## Other Feasibility Issues

**27**

There can be any number of other outside factors which may impact the feasibility of your project. Let's look at a few of them.

## Design and HOA

Be especially alert to design guidelines imposed by community associations. These often create the most aggravation for homeowners. Essentially, design guidelines tell you how your improvement must look – sometimes in very specific terms. Nearly every homeowners' association will have design guidelines which you must comply with, and many municipalities have adopted some sort of guidelines. If you are a member of an association, be sure to obtain a copy of the latest issue of the design guidelines from the property management company or the board of directors. It is usually wise to obtain design approval from your association before proceeding with working drawings or submitting plans to the city for review, and mandatory before commencing construction. Many cities, when dealing with properties subject to HOA review, will not even accept plans for review without receiving a written approval from the association.

City design guidelines are often included in special district guidelines or general plans. Occasionally they will be found in conditions of approval granted to developers and running with the properties within those projects. In other words, a little digging may be necessary to answer the question. Your city planner can help you.

## Utilities

28

If you are building from scratch on a lot you own, you need to determine if basic services are available. These include water, sewer, power and gas. Just the fact that the street is in, and houses have even been built nearby or next door, does not guarantee that services are available. Water and sewer are constrained by capacity. If capacity is at its limit, additional water meters or sewer taps may not be available. In some areas of California, for instance, there are waiting lists many years long for water meters.

An alternative to public sewer service may be a septic system, but these are usually subject to strict regulation by the state health department and often are not feasible. Building without a source of water is impractical, and often prohibited. Electric power is usually not an issue, but gas is frequently unavailable in rural areas.

Utilities may be provided by the city, but often are provided by private companies – such as for electricity, telephone or cable TV – or by special districts formed to provide water or sewer services. Storm drainage is usually a government service, but occasionally you might find a private storm drainage district.

## School Districts

The most significant special districts are school districts. For many homeowners the quality of local schools is of paramount importance. Most schools are rated and those ratings can usually be found online. Not only should you check the quality rating of a school, but be sure the school has adequate capacity, both currently and for the future. School districts also have the power to levy taxes and impact fees. School impact fees usually do not apply to renovation work, but new construction rarely escapes. School fees are usually square footage based. Determine if there is one school district, or separate districts for elementary and high schools. School fees can be significant.

29

## Other Special Districts

Other special districts with taxing authority may include libraries, lighting and streetscaping. The power to collect assessments is often assigned to the building department, although sometimes the fees are paid directly, especially school fees, and a receipt is issued which must be delivered to the building department before a permit can be issued.

Fire regulations are important to be aware of, particularly in rural areas with high fire danger, such as southern California. There may be special requirements for roofing, siding and a defensible perimeter and for fire sprinklers.

## Environmental

If your project is new construction in a rural setting, perhaps on a large parcel you own, there might be wetlands, endangered species or archaeological issues. For most improved vacant lots, and almost every modification to an existing building, you will not need to worry about those types of environmental issues.[5]

## Soils

Likely not something you have considered, but you need to know if the soils on your property are able to support the structure you have in mind. Dirt is not just dirt. Beneath the topsoil (assuming you have topsoil) you can be in for any number of surprises. You could hit solid rock two feet down; or water. The soils could be bentonite (expands when it gets wet) or clay (elastic). Neither will provide good bearing for a building. Are you near an earthquake fault line? To get these answers it may be necessary to have a geotechnical subsoils investigation performed.

## Hazardous Materials

You also need to ascertain whether there is, or has been, any contamination of the soils or if any hazardous wastes have been stored on the property. If you haven't yet purchased the property, you need to have a Phase I environmental investigation done. If contaminants are present, or likely to be present, that's pretty much the end of the deal right there.

If your project involves renovation of a building built before 1980 you will need to test for lead based paints and asbestos. Lead is very toxic, especially to children. Most paints used before 1979, when lead was banned, were lead based and must be removed and disposed of in a controlled manner.

---

[5] As with any project, be sure. A room addition may trigger a waste water re-cycling or xeroscaping requirement, for instance.

Asbestos is a frightening material used, it seems, in just about everything up and into the 1970's including vinyl flooring (floor tiles were known as VAT, vinyl asbestos tile), popcorn ceilings, drywall, drywall finishing compounds, roofing, plaster, insulation and on and on. Undisturbed in place it is not generally a problem, but when disturbed asbestos degrades into fine dust particles which, when inhaled, can lead to cancer. It is very toxic and dangerous and must be treated with special care. Don't mess around.

Asbestos and lead remediation is a highly regulated specialty. Extreme care must be taken with the removal of asbestos due to the highly carcinogenic nature of inhaled fibers. Disposal of asbestos particles is subject to chain of custody rules and asbestos and lead can only be disposed of in approved dump sites. Any removal work should be performed by specially licensed contractors.

31

If your project involves an older building, it is wise to engage a special inspector to inspect for asbestos and lead. You will want to know the extent and determine a cost for remediation. Sometimes the inspection results can be the determining factor whether you proceed with your project or not. Better to know early, before you spend money on plans, or even have begun construction.

# THE BUILDING DEPARTMENT

The building and planning departments have different jobs. While the task of the planning department is to oversee the development of the city, the job of the building department is to assure that what is built is built in accordance with the standards of safety set forth in the building code. The building department receives proposed building plans, reviews those plans for compliance with myriad standards (usually coordinating the review of several departments including fire, traffic, health, sometimes planning, and others); then issues a building permit; conducts inspections during the course of construction; and issues a certificate of occupancy upon completion.

**32**

Building codes developed as a response to the tragic conflagrations that periodically swept through cities of wooden buildings, and to health, welfare and structural issues. Today's building codes have grown to include accessibility, energy and other concerns of modern society.

Sometimes the plans reviewer will require revisions to the plans. Having a well prepared set of plans prior to submittal makes for a smoother review process and a happier building official. Plans reviewers are generally overworked and tend to have little patience with poorly prepared plans.

Having a permit and a certificate of occupancy can be important when it comes time to sell your house. For instance, a buyer's lender may not be willing to lend if improvements are "bootlegged" rather than certified by a certificate of occupancy. Just like your relationship with planning, you will want to maintain a cordial relationship with the plans reviewer and the inspector.

# HELP! DO I NEED A CONSULTANT?

Much of your project research you can do yourself, but there are consultants available who will do it for you. Or you can package the work into a design contract. Certainly, doing the preliminary research yourself will save you significant money and is generally not that difficult, as well as being educational. The more informed you are, the more in control of your project and the process you will be.

## Planning Consultants

33

For help with planning and zoning issues there are expeditors or planning consultants. Type in "planning consultants" or "zoning consultants" in Google. Fees are usually hourly. As of this writing, $75 - $90 per hour is a typical going rate. Any more than that for residential work is excessive. If the research is simple, where the consultant is simply looking up the code for you online, expect to be billed two or three hours. If the research is more complex, including visits downtown, you will pay more. Remember, consultants work by the hour, so the billing will be open ended.

For preliminary research, retaining a consultant may not be necessary. There are certain jurisdictions where a consultant will have experience and insight that makes his or her time well worth the investment. Properties within coastal zone special management areas or involving multiple jurisdictions are good examples. Some towns, especially wealthy resort towns, are known to be extremely difficult to navigate. A few dollars spent early can often make a big difference and will be money extremely well spent.

## Expeditors vs. Planning Consultants

Later, in the Pre-Construction phase, you may elect to retain the services of an expeditor to process your building permit. An expeditor is a specialist in the rules of permitting and building approvals. Originally expeditors were simply plans runners – that is, they were tasked with going to the building department and waiting in line to chase down and complete all the paperwork needed for issuance of a building permit.

As codes have become more complex (or convoluted) the services provided by expeditors have increased. Utilizing their intimate and thorough knowledge of the permitting and approvals processes, many expeditors now serve as planning consultants helping their clients plot a path (hopefully) to tricky or complex approvals. Expeditors give advice not just on the building permit itself, but on zoning, use and other issues – often meeting with city planners early in the process and going as far as appearing before neighborhood boards and planning commission hearings. The distinction between "expeditor" and "planning consultant" has become increasingly blurred.

For projects which are in highly regulated areas, or which are pushing the envelope of what is permitted, the services of a planning consultant or an expeditor can be well worth the expense.

## DON'T BE AFRAID TO ASK FOR HELP:  A Moment of Serendipity

When I was young and fresh out of college, I got my first job in construction as a carpenter's apprentice.  (earning – in 1970 – $3.25 per hour.)  To say I was raw is understating it – I knew absolutely nothing.

To be ready for my first day on the job I needed a hammer, tape measure and tool belt.  (The foreman who hired me was kind enough to give me a list.)  So I went down to the hardware store and purchased a hammer (the wrong kind), a tape measure (too short) and new leather nail-bags.  New leather, of course, is stiff, shiny and very clean.  I realized that I would stand out like a light-bulb walking onto the job site with my new tool kit.  Anticipating my soon to be embarrassment, my first thought was to throw those nail-bags on the ground and stomp on them.  Scruff 'em up a bit.  Luckily my second thought was much better – don't stomp on them.  I left them clean and bright and new and the next day walked on the jobsite proudly wearing my inexperience for all to see.

What I found – just what I had realized in my moment of serendipity the evening before – was that there is no embarrassment in admitting what you don't know.  By admitting my ignorance and freely asking for advice, I found that the gruff old construction veterans were more than happy to share their experience with me.  I realized that had I dirtied my bags and pretended to be what I wasn't, I would not have fooled anyone.  On the contrary, I would have actually brought negative attention to myself, and would have looked the fool for attempting it.  Instead of helping and teaching me, my co-workers would have watched me die on the vine.   But I had earned their respect by simply admitting what I didn't know.

My moral is this:  by realizing what you don't know, and by asking for advice, you will find that those who have the knowledge are very willing to share it – and are more likely to give you a fair shake than if you try to bluff your way through.  Remember, the only dumb question is the one you should have asked, but didn't.

35

feasibility

# design & planning

# THE DESIGN

Now that you have determined that your project is feasible, it's time to start the design and planning of your project.  This section of the book tackles the process of how to go about planning a construction project.  We place the design and planning stage in the context of the entire project and look at all the interfaces; we introduce you to construction drawings and construction documents; we discuss planning options and who might be the right consultant for your project.  We get into how plans are organized and how to read them; we discuss drafting options (such as computer aided design); and we guide you through negotiating and signing a planning agreement.  Finally we give you a design and planning checklist.

We will not talk about design options or components.  We will talk about how to take the first step; who can help you; how you find them; how you hire them, manage them and pay them.

> "Give me six hours to chop down a tree and I will spend the first four sharpening the axe."
> — Abraham Lincoln

The American architect Louis Sullivan, father of the modern skyscraper, is famous for saying that "form follows function."  Good design will respond to your needs and desires.

What is design?  Yes, it is the layout and configuration of the floor plan; and, yes, it is the look of the building.  But it is also the materials from which the project is constructed and the finishes applied to the surfaces. It is the unification of the inside and the outside; flat planes and three dimensions. It is also the wires and pipes; the mechanical and electrical systems that make the building function. Creating unity of all these components is the goal of design. When that unity succeeds, it is aesthetically pleasing; indeed, form follows function.

## Start with an Idea!

**40**

You likely have well established aesthetic tastes – you like modern, or colonial or Victorian. You probably also have some general functionality requirements in mind – more counter space, a bigger bedroom, a baby on the way. Now you need start turning these ideas into a plan.

You have probably designing already – maybe without even realizing it – but it is good at this point to formalize your analysis. Say you are considering a kitchen renovation. Make a list of what you like about your current kitchen, and what you don't. Think about how you would change things – both the layout for function (form follows function), and the look. Think about how you use the space, both as a workspace and as a social space. Consider lighting.

## Visualize your Ideas

Sort through all those magazine clippings you've been saving, and start narrowing down your ideas. Talk to friends whose kitchens you like and find out what works – or what doesn't – in their spaces. Take a pencil and paper and sketch ideas. The more you think about your goals, the clearer your project becomes in your mind. And the clearer your project is to you, the easier it will be to communicate your ideas to your project team.

## Articulate your Ideas

Now that your ideas are starting to become organized into a clearer picture, it is time to begin formalizing your design. Some people have very good spatial sense and are able to articulate their ideas easily on a piece of paper. Other people find that more difficult. Regardless, it is usually time to turn to a professional designer.

**41**

---

### DO I NEED HELP?

Big Project – yes                                    Small Project – again, yes

---

This is your first big decision. There are several options; each, of course, with pros and cons. Often the first question homeowners struggle with is "do I need an architect?" The answer, like so much else in home renovation: "it depends." To answer that question, let's first look at the construction process. Figure 3 (on page 11) is a schematic outline of the entire project process; it visualizes each of the steps involved in bringing a successful project from idea to built.

## THE PLANS

It helps to understand what is required in the way of construction documents for a building project. As you can imagine, a nuclear power station will have a huge and tremendously complex set of plans and documents, while many bathroom remodels have been completed without any drawings or written documents at all. Let's assume your project is going to fall somewhere in between.

**42**

Construction documents, in their broadest sense, consist of working drawings, specifications, the construction contract and the conditions of the contract. There are also a number of corollary and subsidiary documents. We will discuss each in turn, but right now we are going to restrict our discussion to the working drawings, often simply called the "drawings" or the "plans".

## TYPICAL LIST OF CONSTRUCTION DOCUMENTS

- Working Drawings
- Written Specifications
- Request for Bid Proposal (RFP)
- Construction Contract
- General Conditions of Construction
- Special Conditions
- Schedule of Values
- Requests for Information (RFI)
- Addendums to the Plans or Specifications
- Change Orders
- Shop Drawings
- Product Submittals
- Finishes Selections

## OTHER PROJECT DOCUMENTS

- Payment Requests
- Lien Waivers
- Preliminary Notices
- Final Release

43

## BLUEPRINTS

Plans are still often referred to, especially by those of us who began our careers before the computer age, as "blueprints". Blueprinting refers to the method of reproducing plans used before xerography and digital printing.

The blueprinting process was invented by Alphonse Louis Poitevin, a French chemist, in 1861. It is a process of transferring a line drawing by contact to another surface using ultra-violet light. The process results in a negative image of the original – leaving a reverse image with a dark blue background and white lines – hence, blueprint.

In the 1940s a process called diazo became widespread wherein the background and line colors were reversed, resulting in blue lines on a white background. These prints are sometimes referred to as "blueline" prints, but more generally, were still called "blueprints". Both blue methods are susceptible to moisture and sunlight. Thus, plans rained upon or left in the sun could wash or fade away. Modern techniques eliminated these problems, as well as made the reproduction process much faster and more efficient. One benefit is the ability to produce "half size" plans – plans reduced by 50% so that ¼" scale become 1/8" scale, etc. Half size plans are very convenient and easy to unroll and use – sort of like using an tablet versus a desktop.

With the advent of xerography, plans are now simply copied on large format copiers. With the recent widespread use of CAD, prints can be made directly from digital files using either xerography or digital ink plotters. While blueprint and blueline are actual contact reproductions thus exactly reproducing the original in exact scale, xerographic reproductions can be manipulated, thus allowing half-size plans, but also the opportunity for slight variations of scale which must be guarded against. However, they are very easily reproduced anywhere without the necessity of using the original tracings.

Prior to blueprinting construction plans were laboriously hand traced on paper or linen in ink. Erasures were not possible, so the draftsman could not make a single mistake. With the advent of blueprinting, original drawings were made in pencil on transparent paper.

44

# DESIGN OPTIONS – WHO DOES WHAT

All plans begin with an idea, often just a sketch on the back of a napkin. A designer takes this idea and refines it into a design plan, which, when approved by the owner, becomes the basis for the working drawings. The working drawings, when reviewed and approved by the building department, become the "permit set" which are the plans kept on the jobsite and which are the basis for the actual construction of the project.

## Designers

A designer generally limits his or her work to creating spatial layouts and selecting finishes and furnishings. They will help you layout the kitchen, for instance, and select the cabinet style, the countertops and so forth. Most designers do not create working drawings.

Often designers are actually "interior designers", specializing in room finishes. Interior designers have expertise in furniture, furniture placement, lighting, finish materials, fabrics and colors. Because they work so closely with homeowners, interior designers are often asked, or assume the role, of building designer. Many designers work independently to create design solutions which are then turned over to a draftsman or licensed architect to create working drawings.

While some interior designers have very strong building design talents, often they lack understanding of structural, code and other issues that inform final design solutions. Other designers specialize in building design and may have very little to do with interior design issues. There are very talented building designers at work who have virtually all the abilities of licensed architects, but are not, for any number of reasons, licensed architects. These designers may have the ability to create highly sophisticated building designs

**45**

and space plans, but usually lack, or are simply not interested in, the technical expertise in building construction which architects bring to the table.

Designer fees can vary widely and it is best to be very cautious when engaging a designer, as their fees can quickly run out of control.

## Architects

Usually the first option that occurs to most homeowners is to engage the services of a licensed architect. This is the top position in the design hierachy, and the most expensive choice. However, an architect is the most highly trained of all the design professionals, generally delivers the most complete plans and supporting documents, and is usually willing and able provide support through the building process. Architects usually work independently of contractors, but in some instance are associated with design builders.

A person cannot practice as an architect absent being licensed by the state within which he or she is working. To become licensed as an architect, the candidate must – in most cases – have completed a five year degree program at an accredited school of architecture, including course study in theory, design, drafting, structural engineering, materials, mechanical systems and the history of architecture. Before being eligible to sit for the qualifying exam, a candidate must have spent at least of year working as an apprentice under the direction of a licensed architect.[6]

Architects can be engaged to perform a greater or lesser scope of services – from conceptual design through working drawings and building specifications to construction oversight. Many states require the architect of

[6] Some states, California being one, still allow candidates to sit for the licensing exam absent a degree, provided they can document a number of years working in the office and under the direction of a licensed architect.

46

record – that is, the architect who places his license stamp and signature on the plans – to oversee the construction to assure that it complies with the approved drawings and specifications. Plans prepared by licensed architects are accepted by building departments as competent.

Architects' fees usually reflect their level of expertise and years of education, as well as their professional success.

## Draftspersons

An alternative on simpler projects is to engage a draftsperson, who is not licensed as an architect, to create working drawings from your design sketches. Essentially a draftsperson is a technician. Some work on their own; many work for architects and moonlight on the side. Many draftspersons are highly competent and produce plans as good, or even better, than some licensed architects. While their plans drawing and code skills may be excellent, generally they have limited engineering expertise and may, or may not, have aesthetic sensibilities. Given their lack of licensure and more limited professional scope, draftspersons are predictably less expensive to hire than architects. Pricing is often quoted by the page.

## Design Build

An alternative, which is increasingly popular for residential work, is to engage a design/build contractor who will both design the work and build it. The greatest benefit of using design/build is that the D/B contractor is responsible for the entire project. He will be estimating costs not only concurrently with the design work, but under the same roof. This assures that the design solution will match your budget commitment. In addition, he will guarantee to build the project as designed for the budget amount you and he have arrived at. And, being responsible for the design and working drawings,

47

and having guaranteed the budget, he is responsible to resolve and absorb the cost of any errors, oversights or omissions. In other words, you have a built in guarantee against design failures and design failure cost over-runs. Turn to page 116 for a more complete discussion of design/build.

Design/build offers the construction cost certainty which is lacking when plans are prepared independently. We have all heard stories of architects preparing "unbuildable" plans; or plans which come in way over budget when put out for bid and which then must be scrapped – and the money invested is simply written off as a loss.

**48**

On the other hand, going the design/build route requires a commitment prior to knowing the final cost. The final cost is resolved by a collaborative effort between the design/builder and the client. The price is negotiated, rather than competitively bid. It is very much a relationship of trust and confidence in your builder.

## Stock Plans

A final option when contemplating a new home is to purchase a stock plan. A stock plan is a "spec" plan pre-drafted by a draftsman or architect and offered for sale. It is usually licensed for a one time use and is not exclusive to the purchaser. Stock plans can be found online or published in books. There are thousands of stock plans available in all styles and sizes. Most now come digitally for easy reproduction. Many come with materials lists; some publishers offer customization of their plans. Or you can take a stock plan to a designer or architect for modification. A word of caution – the foundation design will likely need to be a site specific design, which would be a cost in addition to the base plans purchase price. You would need to engage an architect or structural engineer for this work.

## Be Aware of Building Department Requirements

You will need to understand the requirements of your local building department if you elect to use only a designer or a draftsperson. Many building departments require that plans be prepared, or, at a minimum, reviewed by a licensed architect or structural engineer who must stamp the plans with his or her professional stamp and sign them.[7] This is not always the case, or may apply only to certain portions of the plans. Your local building department will be able to give you guidance. Most building departments will have a "plans submittal" checklist which you can usually find online.

## The Right Choice

What, you are asking, is the right choice for me. Again, it depends – usually upon the size and scope of your project. Generally, the smaller and simpler the project, the less need to engage extensive and expensive architectural services. Most of us will agree that re-doing the kitchen cabinets and countertops and maybe new lighting probably does not demand a multi-page set of plans and specifications. On the other hand, if the work involves re-configuring the kitchen, knocking out exterior walls and doubling the size of the room, you may well feel that an architect is the right choice. The larger and more complex the project, the more sophisticated will be the planning and design skills needed.

---

[7] The signature on the plans set (or sets) submitted to the building department for review typically must be an original signature in ink applied to each page *after* the plans pages are printed. This ensures that the representations in the plans are exactly those reviewed and approved by the signer. Otherwise it is possible to make changes to the drawings after the signature is applied. This application of an original signature in ink is called a "wet signature". The stamp application must also be "wet".

If you have a strong vision of your design, maybe the right choice is a draftsman who will simply translate your vision onto paper. If you are unable to envision your project clearly, you will likely need the services of a designer and/or an architect. In more complex projects, the right choice may be multiple choices – planning consultant, designer and an architect.

Put your project ideas down on paper – reducing anything to writing clarifies your thinking and organizes your thoughts. Start by stating your goal; then set down what you have resolved, and what you haven't. Refer back to the four phases of a building project; and then look at the Project Process Chart. Identify your strengths, and where you need help. Be realistic.

**50**

## CHOOSING A DESIGN CONSULTANT

### Sorting through the Candidates

When you reach a decision about where you need to engage help – and what type – it's time to find that help.

If you know anyone who has completed a remodel or new home project, start there. Ask them how they proceeded and who they used. Find out what they liked about the process (and the person they used) and what they didn't like. Ask them what they would do differently next time.

Go online and search for designers and architects in your area and visit their websites. Check out design/builders. I like to see how well the websites are designed – my theory being that if the website is well-designed, well-organized and informative, then that is a reflection of their professional performance. Look at their portfolios. Is there a sufficient – it need not be exhaustive; that can be too much – selection of projects so that you can get a sense of their quality and style? Have they posted their picture and biography. I like to see who I am considering and what they look like. I also want to know specifics about them and their career, not some boiler plate. Have they posted testimonials? (Of course, nobody posts a bad review.)

Drive around. Look for projects under construction; the architect and builder will both have their signs posted. If you like the look of the project, jot their names down. You can also go to the building department and take a look at the building permit record.

Also, there is no need to start with the architect or designer selection; you can first choose your contractor and ask him to recommend an architect or designer.

One last word of caution – do not hire friends or family. There will be moments of tension on any project; you do not want a disagreement on your project to color your personal relationships. Remember, as soon as you hire someone it is no longer a relationship of equals.

## What Should You Be Looking For?

A good first step is to check with the Better Business Bureau – is your candidate a member? Are they complaint fee; or – and we all have complaints – if there is a complaint, how was it resolved. Check Angie's list (caveat – Angie's list often has only one or two comments apiece, not really enough to rely on alone). Check Yelp!, but take it with a grain of salt.

After you select candidates – and don't overwhelm yourself; try to keep the list relatively short – it is time to visit each one. While you are interviewing them, they will likewise be interviewing you. You both need a good fit.

51

---

### TRUST AND CONFIDENCE

You should avoid choosing a builder, or an architect, or any other member of your project team based solely on price. Home remodeling or building a custom home is an intimate project and you are going to have an intimate relationship with your team members. You want to start the project with trust, have your confidence be validated throughout the project, and be friends at the end.

Consider if any possible cost savings are worth sacrificing any portion of your comfort level to achieve.

---

**52**

The first question – before you even make the appointment – is to ascertain if they do the type of project you are doing. If not, go on to the next candidate.

I like to start with small talk – this tells me right away if I am talking with (notice I didn't say "to") someone I can be comfortable with. This is critical. You will be involved with this person for several months, in a fairly intimate way and probably through a number of stressful situations. A building project is challenging enough without adding the difficulty of an awkward or uncomfortable relationship with one of your key team members. You don't need to be barroom buddies, but you want to be comfortable.

Does he or she listen to you; are you willing to listen to him or her? Is he or she respectful of your ideas and opinions; do you like what they have to say? Are they well-grounded; or are they full of themselves? Have a set of questions to ask; ask what questions they have of you. You have to be comfortable with and settle into your choice. Even if the first candidate you visit feels right, keep two or three more appointments. Be sure.

A word of caution – everyone is at their most charming during the first meeting, but try to get a general read. How "nice" the person is when you meet them is important, but how nice the person is at those awkward moments later on is more important. To determine that you will need to dig deeper.

Ask for recent references – both homeowners and contractors – and contact them. Have a set list of questions to ask each; then compare the answers. Check with the Better Business Bureau for complaints and, if any, how they were resolved (not all complaints are valid). Verify their license – is it current; have there ever been professional complaints or disciplinary actions. Check the records of superior court to discover any litigation history.

**53**

The hardest answer to figure out is this one: is everything going to be an extra. That is, if it is not specifically provided for in the contract, are you going to be charged for it. In some ways, a contract written with short, but broad language, is your best assurance that you are covered. A contract written to the last detail can use that specificity as proof of intent as to what was included. If it is not part of the list of many specific things, then it was an omission on purpose and never intended to be included. On the other hand, if the language is general, you can have an argument about what is standard practice to be included, and to what degree. The words "and the like" and "anything else necessary to thoroughly complete the task contemplated by this agreement" are good phrases to include in any contract.

## QUESTIONS TO ASK YOUR DESIGN PROFESSIONAL

### Background

- How long  have you been doing this
- From which school did you graduate
- Why did you choose this career
- Who is your greatest professional influence and why
- What was your first job
- Have you ever worked as a construction worker
- What is your favorite project you have ever done
- What was the most challenging job you have ever done
- What kind of input do you like from your clients
- What is your ideal client

### Executing the Work

- How extensive a set of plans do you think this project requires
- How extensive a set of specs
- Will you personally be performing the work
- If not, who; what are their qualifications; can we meet them
- How do you prefer to structure your fee – fixed, cost-plus or hourly
- How do you handle finishes selections and specifications
- Who owns the plans; if he does, what are your rights
- Will he give you a digital file of the plans and specs
- How's their workload – do they have the time for you that you want

## QUESTIONS TO ASK YOUR DESIGN PROFESSIONAL (cont.)

### References

- What do you like in a contractor
- May we talk to some contractors you have worked with recently
- May we talk to some homeowners you have worked with recently
- What happens if we have a disagreement
- What is the most common cause of discord on a residential project
- Are you a member of AIA
- Are you a member of Better Business Bureau
- Have you ever been in a fee dispute
- Have you ever been in a dispute or litigation about your work

### Fixed Fee Questions

- How many client meetings are included
- How many design revisions are included
- How extensive are the drawings; what type and how many details – please show me a typical set
- How thorough are the written specifications
- Do you include a certificate of completion

### Construction Oversight Questions

- How often do you visit the site
- Who conducts the visit
- What is their experience
- How do you assure quality
- Do you review and approve payment requests
- Do you prepare written reports and photographic record

55

## Computer Aided Design (CAD)

First, eliminate anyone who does not use CAD.  CAD stands for computer aided design.  Although there may be a few talented designers around still working by hand, virtually the entire building design world now works in CAD.  The virtues of CAD are many:  precision, ease of revision, digital transmission, collaboration, ease of reproduction.  A designer who is able to layout a design in CAD can transmit the design instantly to the architect who is able to use the same digital file as the basis for the architectural plans.  The architect then forwards the drawings to the structural engineer who is able to use the same files to create his structural drawings.  All the parties are able to instantly exchange revisions which can populate all pages at the same time.  Anyone who has a copy of the file can make modifications to the plans.[8]  Finally, digital sets of the plans, or just the appropriate pages, can be emailed to multiple construction bidders for estimating purposes.  During construction, revisions can be easily and accurately communicated nearly instantly.

56

---

[8] This, of course, can be both a convenience and a curse.   The great advantage is the ability of plans to, in a sense, become "open source", in that anyone with access to the file can create a modification without the lengthy process of going back to the original set.  Of course, the danger is just that – anyone can change the drawings.  This is the key reason for wet stamping plans (discussed in the previous footnote).

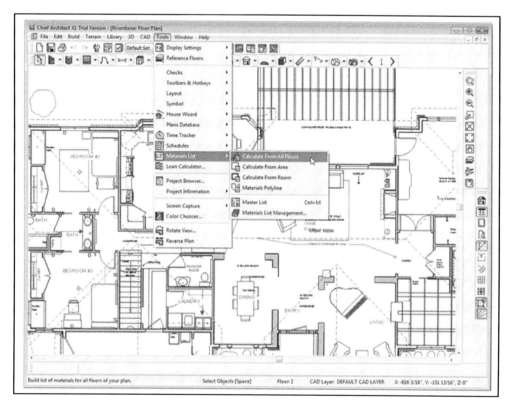

Figure 6: This is a screenshot from a CAD software program showing various commands. The drafter is working on a residential floorplan. Visible are walls, windows, doors and furniture placement. This is one layer of several, including a second floor plan, roof plan and foundation plan.

There are multiple CAD programs. The industry standard is AutoCAD published by AutoDesk. AutoDesk publishes CAD programs tailored to architecture and structural engineering, civil engineering and to mechanical and electrical users, as well as for many industrial applications. In recent years AutoDesk has led the way into BIM, short for building image modeling. BIM is the ability to draw plans in three dimensions, rather than two dimensionally. This allows clearer understanding of volumes during the design process.

Although very powerful design tools, CAD has a steep the learning curve. The basic AutoCAD file format (.dwg) is recognized and accepted by most architectural design software programs[9].

Figure 7: This drawing is an example of building image modeling. It is drawn in three dimensions rather than in two dimensions, on a flat plane. This allows a clear understanding of what is going on above, below and on all sides simultaneously as an element is being drawn. Digital programs can place furniture and even perform automatic materials takeoffs.

There are other architectural software programs which are popular. They have varying degrees of sophistication and popularity. While AutoCAD

---

[9] The other most widely used file format is .dxf.

was originally created as a universal CAD program, these other programs were designed specifically for drawing buildings. Among the most widely used residential programs are SoftPlan and Chief Architect. Both are highly evolved programs. Both have powerful rendering tools which allow for the creation of 3-D renderings, including the creation of "tours" – the ability to walk through the rooms of a building virtually, including the placement of furniture, surface finishes and colors. These are powerful visualization tools for the homeowner trying to understand exactly what the finished product will look like.

There are also a number of cabinet design programs (the most popular is 20-20) and simple home design and room layout programs designed for consumer use. These simple room layout programs can be found online after a quick search.

Regardless of the program used, the files should be created in, or convertible to, either .dwg or .dxf. Be sure that any work you commission will be delivered to you in one of these file formats, preferably .dwg.

Although I've recommended eliminating from consideration anyone who does not work in CAD, I'm going to back off that a little bit. If you find a designer whose work you like, and with whom you are comfortable, who does not work in CAD – that's OK. Design concepts often start as a hand drawing, and there are many, usually older, talented designers who still work exclusively by hand. Many of them have wonderful rendering skills and create beautiful hand drawn renderings. Just understand that for projects of any size or complexity, hand drawings will need to be converted which will involve additional expense. Working drawings should always be in CAD.

# PRELIMINARY DESIGN

Preliminary or conceptual design is where you turn an idea into a concept. The goal is to firm up the idea without worrying too much yet about precision and details. Dimensions are approximate. The object is to work out how the changes will fit with the existing building when remodeling, or how a new house will fit on the lot, use available views, respond to its environment. You are thinking about how you will use the space or spaces – revising the work flow in a kitchen, for instance, or how your family functions within your home.

**60**

Thought is given to how much room you need, and how much room you are allowed by code. This is when the initial trade-offs begin between what you want, what you can afford or what the zoning code will allow. Consideration is given to views, sunlight and other environmental issues. Where do you want windows; where to put the television; how will furniture fit in the rooms.

As the design begins to take shape, you begin to refine the details. You will consider exterior and interior finishes. At this point it is wise to consider cost impacts of different design choices[10].

Many designers will prepare a rendered floorplan; that is, a sketch plan into which they have dropped furniture placements and colored the different features, such as flooring types, so that it is easy to visualize the layout. Many will also prepare perspective renderings to help their clients visualize what the finished structure or room will look like.

---

[10] This is a perfect example of an argument for using design/build.

 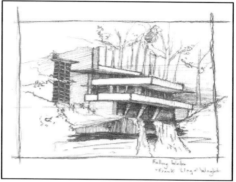

Figure 8: These are three of the most famous concept sketches of all time – Frank Lloyd Wright's famous Fallingwater house in Bear Run, Pennsylvania. They follow the great architect's evolving design.

# WORKING DRAWINGS

Once you have refined your design ideas and settled upon a solution, it is time to turn the design sketches or plans into architectural, or "working", drawings. The architectural drawings are the detailed, dimensioned and accurate drawings which are used to guide the contractor and subcontractors as they build the project, and which are used to create the construction cost estimate.

While design drawings work out the concept, architectural drawings set forth precisely how a building is to be built. Architectural drawings are fully dimensioned, all openings are sized and materials and finishes are specified. How the parts are connected is detailed and all code compliance is resolved.

The architectural drawings follow a regular system or organization with a presentation order and page numbering protocol which is generally consistent in all residential plans. The plans are organized into sections which are designated by a letter, followed by a number which counts the pages in the section. For example, the first page of the architectural section would be page A-1, followed by A-2, etc. Each page also is given a written title such as "Main Floor Plan" or "Building Section". Often it becomes necessary or convenient to insert additional pages, in which case the inserted page(s) would be numbered A-1.1, A-1.2, etc.

# HOW CONSTRUCTION PLANS ARE ORGANIZED

A typical plans set for a new house will consist of title page(s), civil pages, architectural pages, structural pages, mechanical pages, electrical pages and perhaps landscape pages. Occasionally plans will also include decorating pages. The lettering for these sections is as follows:

T: Title pages. When a plans set consists of only one title page it often appears as the first page in the set without a page number. As the approvals process has become more complex, increasing amounts of information are required to be set forth on the plans such as zoning disclosures, energy calculations, water usage, special inspection requirements, conditions of approval, etc. These often require more than one page.

C: Civil pages. The civil page(s) contain the location map, site plan, grading and drainage plan, temporary stormwater mitigation plan and utility services information. Civil refers to civil engineering, which is the technical design of grading, roads and utilities – anything involving the surface of the earth or below.[11]

**63**

A: Architectural pages. These pages contain the actual building construction drawings which usually consist of the floor plan(s), exterior elevations, building sections, foundation plan, roof plan, perhaps a reflected ceiling plan, and details.

S: Structural pages: The word "structural" may be most readily understood as referring to the frame (or skeleton) of a building. New construction and projects involving structural modifications will likely require that the design of the structural elements – a such as foundations, beams, posts and connections –be designed by a licensed structural engineer. These pages typically consist of plans drawings, sections, details, nailing patterns and other information important for the structural work. Calculations are often attached as an exhibit when submitted for plan review.

M: Mechanical pages. These are the plumbing and air conditioning drawings. Usually plan view drawings, they may also include piping schematics and fixtures schedules.

---

[11] In construction slang, often called "horizontal" as opposed to "vertical" construction, which refers to buildings from the ground up.

E:  Electrical pages.  Usually plan view drawings, they may also include a "one line" drawing showing the configuration of the service equipment, distribution circuits and shutoffs.  A lighting list may be included.

L:  Landscaping pages.  Usually a plan view showing the plant layout, sprinkler design and plants schedule.

Some jurisdictions require additional miscellaneous pages, usually included either in the title section, or at the end of the set, which might include photographs of the existing structure in the instance of a remodeling project, sunlight and shadow studies, streetscape images, etc.

64

Let's look at the plans sections in more detail.

## Civil Pages

The civil pages provide information on the project site.  Included will be a location map which shows where the property is located (basically a street map with the major cross streets and the lot location identified).  For interior remodel projects this is usually sufficient information for the plans checker.

For new construction, room additions or major renovations a site (or plot) plan will be required.  This consists of a survey map of the property with the existing and proposed improvements outlined in place.  Site plans will always have a north arrow and indicate the building location, property lines, the set-back distance of improvements from the property lines and will usually show the location of utility services, connection points and meter locations.  Also shown on site plans are easements, driveways, patios, sidewalks, curb lines, swimming pools, fences, walls and major landscape elements.

The property boundary lines are shown with a long dash/short dash bold line. Properly drawn, next to the lines will appear the compass bearing in degrees, minutes and seconds and the length of the line.

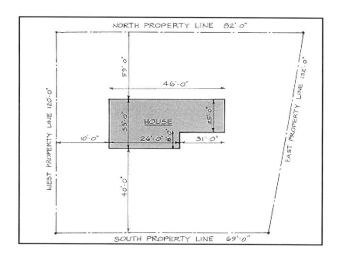

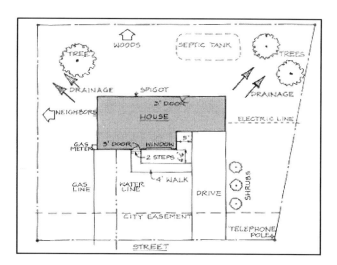

Figure 9: These are very simple examples of site plans.
A more fully realized site plan is shown in the next figure.

Sometimes a grading and drainage plan is incorporated with the site plan; other times it may be a separate drawing. The grading plan will show the existing grade and the proposed new grades using contour lines typically spaced at one, two or five foot intervals. Drainage flows are indicated as well as drain inlets and drain lines. For new work the building department will usually require a calculation of the amount of excavation and fill in cubic yards. More and more building departments are also requiring erosion control plans. Typically they require that grading, drainage and erosion control plans be prepared by a licensed civil engineer. These plans can require the calculation of rainwater runoff – with a typical requirement being that any increase of runoff due to building improvements must be retained on site or discharged into the public storm sewer at no greater than historic rates.

66

Increases in storm runoff due to development are a serious concern both for environmental reasons and for flood control. Many cities have experienced disastrous flooding because planning from 50 or 100 years ago failed to adequately address the concentrated accumulation of rainwater in heavy rainfall events.

Another concern is to maintain the purity of our rivers and lakes by assuring that storm runoff does not pick up pollutants from parking lots, fertilized lawns or other sources of potential contamination. State and federal laws virtually assure that every city have in place policies that address these issues.

During plans review the city's engineering department will review the civil page(s) to assure that any proposed improvements meet the requirements of the city regarding these issues. In addition, most grading will require a separate grading permit and payment of a grading permit fee. Projects involving the stripping of topsoil are of special concern. In order to prevent erosion runoff you may be required to install erosion control fences and inlet protections. These will be shown on the plans as part of the erosion control section.

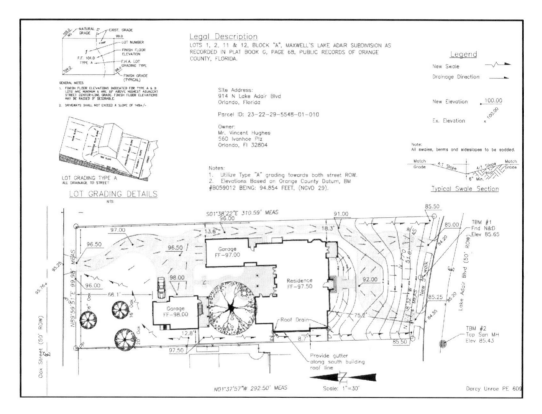

Figure 10: This is an excellent example of a grading plan. The proposed (or existing) building is clearly drawn; the existing grades are shown in faded solid lines with elevations noted; the new proposed contours are clearly shown with elevations also notated. The drainage flow is shown with short, straight arrows and proposed swales are also shown. Main landscaping features are shown, as well as spot grade call-outs. The finish floor elevation of the building and garage are noted. The property boundaries are clearly shown and described.

## Architectural Pages

The primary page in a set of plans is the **Floor Plan**. This is the basis of all the other drawings. The architectural floor plan is a horizontal view (or "plan" view) of a floor of a building; essentially a map of the building. There will be a separate floor plan for each level of a building, including the basement. The floor plan sets forth the limits of the building (exterior walls); delineates the rooms (interior walls or partitions); indicates openings (doors and windows); and provides other information, such a floor coverings, plumbing fixture locations and cabinet layouts.

Similar to the floor plan is the **Roof Plan**, which is a plan view of the roof. The roof plan will show the ridgeline(s), hips and valleys, and edge of fascia and gutters. It shows the type of roof to be constructed, such as gable, hip, flat or some combination. The roofing material will also be called out.

The **Foundation Plan** is a plan view of the structural footings which support the building. On simple buildings, the foundation plan will often be part of the architectural pages. More complex foundations will simply be outlined in the architectural pages, deferring to the structural design pages for construction information and specifications.

Many fancier projects will include a **Reflected Ceiling Plan**. This plan is a mirror image of the floor plan showing the ceiling of each room. The reflected ceiling plan will show the location of light fixtures, air handling vents, crown moldings and recesses, vaults, coffers and other ceiling design features.

Plans pages are typically drawn in ¼" = 1'0" scale, commonly referred to as "quarter scale". Plans pages will have references to enlarged drawings called "details" which are typically located on special "details pages". The protocol for details is discussed below.

It's easier to fix a mistake with an eraser than with a nail puller.

The **Exterior Elevations** are often the most interesting pages because they are a picture of what the building will look like when built. Typically there are four exterior views: front, rear, left and right sides. More complex buildings will have additional views.

The exterior elevations are also usually drawn in quarter scale, although sometimes eighth scale (1/8" = 1'0") is used. The views are drawn flat, without perspective, which sometimes makes reading recesses or projections (or "popouts") more difficult, although sometimes the draftsman will apply shadows. Exterior finish materials are called out, such as stucco or wood siding, the roof pitch and materials, and exterior trim information. The height of the building is shown, as well as the adjacent finish grades. Elevations are fairly simple drawings.

**Sections** are drawings of a more technical nature and are used to illustrate vertical measurements and how the building comes together from a construction standpoint. Sections are vertical slices through a building, either cross ways or longitudinally, placed to reveal the interior placement of floors, beams and other elements. The slice is complete from foundation to roof. Most sets of plans for a house will include more than one section, placed at different critical parts of the building. Remodeling projects often do not require sections.

Sections are lettered, rather than numbered; *i.e.,* Section A-A, Section B-B, etc. Locations are indicated on the plans pages by a line across the plan with the section letter and a plans page reference indicating on which page the section drawing can be found. Section references may also occur on elevations drawings, and even on other sections.

69

The reference shown tells the user to turn to plans page A-6 where the A-A section line drawn through the plan would be displayed as a full vertical section drawing. The view direction is looking in the direction the triangles are pointing. Section drawings are usually drawn in ½" = 1'0" or 3/8" = 1'0" scale.

70

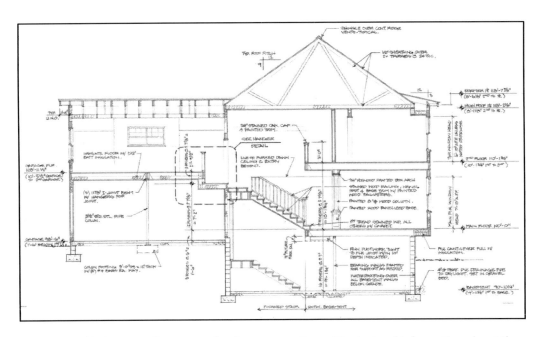

Figure 11: This is an excellent example of a cross section with plenty of information about the way the house is to be constructed, materials used, height measurements and other useful information.

**Details** are enlarged drawings of portions of the main pages. For instance, the ¼" = 1'0" scale is often too small to clearly show certain things, such as how a window sill is to be built or how a beam is connected to a wall. If the draftsman desires to show an element in more detail, he or she will draw a circle around the element with a reference code similar to that used for sections. The reference will direct the plans user to a page on the plans (called a "details page") and to a drawing on that page (called a "detail"). Details may be either numbered or lettered. A typical detail reference would look like this:

$$\frac{5}{A\text{-}10}$$

meaning that the user should turn to page A-10 and refer to detail number 5 on that page.

Details may be taken from any page or drawing on the plans, including other details. Details may be drawn in a number of scales, the most common being 3/8, half, ¾ and one inch.

Finally, the architectural pages must identify and comply with all building code requirements.

## Structural Pages

**Structural** drawings are the engineering solutions and instructions for constructing the foundation and the frame of a building. For example, a designer may design a living space with a large, expansive opening overlooking a dramatic scenic view. He may show it as, say, thirty feet wide without any intermediate supports. The architect may then resolve that same opening as being a stacking, frameless glass sliding door and specify a brand and actual dimensions for the opening to be built. But he doesn't tell the builder what size of beam is needed to span the opening.

That problem is given to the structural engineer who will calculate the beam type and size required to span the opening. He will calculate the weight of all loads on the beam (both the structure above and any objects or people in the building when occupied) , wind loads (the pressure of wind against the building) and seismic resistance required. He will be constrained by the amount of depth (vertical distance) he has within which the beam must fit. Then he will determine the beam type (timber, steel, laminated), the deflection (how much the beam will sag of its own weight) and the size beam needed. He will also specify how the beam is to be connected to the posts which hold it in place, and the size of those posts. And he must calculate the size and strength of the footing which supports the entire assembly.

Structural drawings are often more schematic in appearance than architectural drawings, due to their technical purpose, with simple lines often representing shapes the architect would draw to dimension. They often include a number of pages of "standard" details, some or even most of which may not apply to the particular project at hand. (Most engineers have pre-prepared these details to address common conditions regularly seen in most light construction.) Also included are schedules for reinforcing steel, nailing, special inspections and other applicable requirements. Often the engineer is required to submit his calculations along with the drawings. Usually these are attached on 8.5 x 11 pages separate from the drawings.

On simple buildings the architect may feel comfortable performing his own engineering; but on most buildings he will use the services of a licensed consulting engineer. Usually the structural engineering consultant is contracted by the architect and not directly by the owner. Simple home renovations often do not require any structural engineering.

Typical structural pages include foundations, floor systems, wall systems and roof structure. Often roofs are specified to be constructed using trusses, in which case the roof engineering will be in the form of **Truss**

**Drawings** prepared by the truss manufacturer. There are now sophisticated computer programs which are used to prepare truss drawings and calculate the necessary design loads. These drawings are prepared by a structural engineer specializing in truss design and may be submitted at the time of the plans review, or may be submitted at a later date prior to installation. The cost of truss drawings is usually included in the bid price for the trusses themselves.[12]

## Mechanical, Electrical and Plumbing Pages (MEP)

The mechanical and electrical pages (sometimes called MEP for mechanical, electrical and plumbing) deal with the heating, cooling and plumbing requirements of a building. Most house plans seldom have separate mechanical pages, but should have a separate electrical plan. The plumbing is indicated on the floor plans by placing symbols for toilets, sinks, etc., where they are intended to go. The site plan will show the water and sewer service locations.[13]

73

Mechanical plans address heating and cooling systems, including furnaces (usually a gas fired forced air unit, or FAU), air conditioning equipment and ductwork. While it is not uncommon for plans to be completed, and pass through plans review, without separate mechanical drawings, attention needs to be paid to sizing and location of equipment and ducts. For instance, ducts and pipes must go around, not through, structural elements such as posts and beams; sufficient space must be allowed in floors and walls to accommodate properly sized ducts. Vents from gas fired appliances must

---

[12] It's jumping again, but this is a good time to note that truss bids usually include delivery to the jobsite, but do not include unloading or loading onto the building. Framing bids may, but usually do not include, off-loading or loading onto the roof. Be careful it you are self-contracting that you clarify these tasks in your bid documents.

[13] Be sure who is assigned the task of locating these items – both physically at the property – and on the plans.

have minimum clearances to combustible materials (such as wood framing). Both vertical and horizontal ducting must have clear paths; drains and vents can't show up in the middle of the room above or below. A common mistake is to locate a furnace in the basement without following the path of the vertical vent through to the roof.

Similar attention must be paid to toilets and plumbing drains. While some penetrations can be made in structural elements, these cuts are strictly limited. And remember the cardinal rule of plumbing (paraphrased): liquid flows downhill.

# 74 SPECIFICATIONS

Specifications are created in tandem with the working drawings. While the drawings are a picture of what is to be built, the specifications are the instructions about how to build what is shown in the drawings. Sometimes the "specs" are set forth as written notes on the plans pages; other times they are a separate booklet. They can be very detailed and technical, or they can be of a more general nature. Discuss with your architect what level of thoroughness is appropriate for your project. Regardless, don't waste time creating specs for work which does not occur in your project; also, some sections may warrant more detail than others.

## All the Things That Go Into Your House

In a typical new house project, there are at least 25 distinct trades or categories of work and likely over 100 individual tradesmen on site during the course of the job. This is a typical list of tasks in an average house:

### TRADES IN A TYPICAL HOUSE

| | |
|---|---|
| Surveyor | Sheetmetal and flashing |
| Earthwork and excavation | Waterproofing |
| Underground utility services | Stucco |
| Concrete foundations and rebar | Insulation |
| Retaining walls | Drywall |
| Masonry | Painting |
| Structural steel | Garage doors |
| Rough framing | Swimming pool |
| Roof trusses | Plumbing |
| Crane | Fire sprinklers |
| Windows and sliding doors | Electrical |
| Heating, ventilation and air conditioning | |
| Skylights | Entertainment systems |
| Roofing | Landscaping |

## Master Format

All this work is managed by organizing it according to a system called MasterFormat[14] which is published and curated by the Construction Specifications Institute; and by the project schedule.[15] (Many smaller projects, such as kitchen or bath remodels, use modified versions of MasterFormat which eliminate the non-applicable sections. Regardless, some system of organization is essential.)

Master format is divided into 16 divisions, and numerous sub-sections thereof. The divisions are

| | |
|---|---|
| I. | General Conditions |
| II. | Earthwork |
| III. | Concrete |
| IV. | Masonry |
| V. | Metals |
| VI. | Wood and Plastics |
| VII. | Thermal and Moisture Protection |
| VIII. | Doors and Windows |
| IX. | Finishes |
| X. | Specialties |
| XI. | Equipment |
| XII. | Furnishings |
| XIII. | Special Construction |
| XIV. | Conveying Systems |
| XV. | Mechanical Systems |
| XVI. | Electrical |

---

[14] An alternative system is UniFormat. See the box on the following page.

[15] The Project Schedule will be discussed in the Pre-Construction section of this book.

Of these 16 divisions, divisions XIII and XIV are not seen in most residential projects. Several divisions include a number of trades, such as division IX which includes drywall, flooring, painting, tile and plaster among others.[16]

Some trades have rough and finish phases. The plumber must first install drain lines in the ground under any concrete slabs or foundations to be poured. The pipes are stubbed up and left to be connected later. After the rough structural framing is completed, the plumber will return to complete the "rough in" including drain lines, vent lines and service water piping. Again, these lines are stubbed out and capped to be revisited later. When the house is nearly complete the plumber returns once again to install the finish fixtures – toilets, sinks, etc.

77

This bifurcation, or tri-furcation, of the work of a trade is not reflected in the organization scheme of MasterFormat. For that reason many residential builders will use a modified system of organizing their work which recognizes three separate activities for plumbing, two for electrical, and so forth. The builder will arrange his work by time-line sequence, rather than by trade or construction assembly. This allows for easier scheduling setup and clearer tracking of billings. I have long been a fan of this type of organization.

Each of the divisions is organized into general conditions, standards of execution and specifications of materials. For instance, typical standards to be found in division III, Concrete, would require that all concrete slabs be level to within 1/8" within 8' horizontally, describe the surface finish on various concrete surfaces, and specify the mix ratios of concrete to be placed in the foundations and slabs. The information contained in a well written set of

---

[16] In 2004, MasterFormat was reorganized to recognize advances in building technologies and systems, however the pre-2004 version is much simply and easier to use for most smaller residential projects.

specifications can be an invaluable guide for the construction-unfamiliar to help them assess the performance of the work on their project.

Complete specifications for over 500 sections of MasterFormat can be downloaded for free at http://www.arcat.com/sd/specifications.shtml. The amount of information here is very thorough, but probably intimidating for the average homeowner. However, you can use it to check-up on anything your architect or contractor is telling you about what is an acceptable standard of work. MasterFormat can be purchased at www.csinet.org.

If you have engaged an architect, he or she should include a MasterFormat set of specifications as part of his work product. Be sure to include that in the scope of work in his or her contract. If you have elected to go the design/build route, insist a set of standard specifications be a part of the construction documents. Do not let any reluctance on their part deter you. Anyone not willing to be bound by specifications and standards of performance should automatically be scratched from your list of acceptable service providers.

For an expanded breakdown of MasterFormat see Appendix A.

---

## UNIFORMAT

An alternative organization system called UniFormat is preferred by many building professional for its simpler and more logical scheme of organization. Regardless of the format, it is highly recommended that any construction project be organized using one of these systems.

---

## MASTER FORMAT

MasterFormat is the generally accepted standard for defining the categories of work on a construction project.

The MasterFormat takes a potentially chaotic process – building construction – and organizes it, making the bidding and building process more orderly. Standardizing the presentation of project information improves communication and reduces confusion, omissions and the chance of error.

Prior to World War II the building process lacked a generally accepted system for organizing the work, the specifications or the bidding process. Spurred by wartime innovations, building methods and materials were rapidly advancing and becoming more sophisticated. To bring consistency to the management of the construction processes the Construction Specifications Institute was founded in 1948 and, in 1963, published the first organizational format for managing construction. The name MasterFormat was first used in 1973.

MasterFormat was initially set up as 16 divisions that represent the entire construction process, beginning with Division I: General Conditions, and ending with Division 16: Electrical Systems. These divisions are essentially a table of contents used to organize written specifications, project manuals, bid documents and written contracts. They are also used to assemble and track cost data, to file product information and other technical data, and to identify objects on drawings.

Each division and section is divided into general conditions, products, and execution – setting the standards to be followed when providing the work governed by the division or section.

In 2003 MasterFormat added additional divisions to recognize advances in construction technology, especially in electrical, data and communications systems. However, for smaller residential projects many architects and builders continue to use the simpler, pre-2003 format.

An alternative organization system called UniFormat is preferred by many building professional for its simpler and more logical scheme of organization. Regardless of the format, it is highly recommended that any construction project be organized using one of these systems.

79

# THE BUILDING PERMIT

When they are completed, plans will be submitted to the building department for plan check. Plan check is a review of the drawings by the department for compliance with the building codes. The codes include the building code, plumbing code, electrical code, mechanical code, energy code and fire code. It is important to know, when preparing the plans, which code or codes have been adopted by your jurisdiction. Remember, codes are the minimum standards; in many cases a stricter solution may be appropriate. Plans submitted for review must be certified by the plans preparer by his or her signature. If the building official requires that the plans, or certain sections of them, be prepared by an architect or an engineer, then those pages must be stamped with that person's license stamp and be signed. The stamp and signature must be wet – that is, original ink, not a copy. You will need to submit at least two sets – one to receive back and one for the building official's records.

80

## History

Until 1980 there were a number of codes widely used in the United States. Most of the south relied upon the code published by the Southern Conference of Building Officials, while the western states used the Uniform Building Code. Much of the northeast adopted the National Building Code, state developed codes and the International Building Code. These codes were all "model codes", which meant they lacked the force of law unless adopted by local jurisdictions. Often, when a model code is adopted, the adopting jurisdiction will add to or modify sections of the code to respond to local conditions or concerns of the building official. For instance, mountain communities in Colorado have snow load concerns which communities in Florida could care less about; while Florida towns have hurricane concerns which mean nothing to mountain towns.

## International Residential Code

In 1990 the International Residential Code ("IRC") began to be widely substituted for the early variety of codes in an effort to bring consistency to building practices throughout the country. Today few jurisdictions use codes that are not IRC based.

Check with your local building department for a plans submittal checklist and fee schedule. This can often be done online.

## Plan Check

Expect your plans to spend a greater or lesser amount of time in plan check. The quality of the drawings will have some effect, but mostly it is a question of workload. Rarely will plans come back in less than two or three weeks; sometimes much longer. Some jurisdictions allow private plan checking for a fee: if you are willing to pay, the department will allow the plans to be reviewed by an approved, independent consultant. Some larger, more complex commercial plans are routinely sent out.

81

## Approved Plans Set

When you receive your plans back you will likely find them covered with stamp marks. These address typical issues that the plans checkers find on a regular basis, such as energy conservation requirements, special inspections, recent code changes, or topics of special interest to that building department. The plans may also have redlined corrections. Redlines supersede the plans as drawn and must be followed in the field. There may be sheets of standard requirements stapled to the plans.

The plans you receive back will be the official jobsite set. They must be kept on the jobsite at all times. In recent years building departments have been perforating the pages of the jobsite set with a coded pattern. This assures that the set on the jobsite is the actual set approved, not a copy to which unapproved modifications may have been made. Although you may make a copy – and should – take good care of the originals. Many builders make one or more copies of the approved original set and use a copy for day to day use on the jobsite, thus protecting the permit set from damage. Also, the permit set should not be marked up, while markings and notes on the copied set aren't a problem. You must, however, have the original permit set available on site at all times.

## Permit Fees

Upon completion of review, the building official will calculate the permit fee based upon the estimated value of construction. This is usually based upon a standard cost per square foot which is reviewed annually by the department. You may be surprised to find that permit fees are only one of many fees levied at the time of permit issuance. Be prepared for some heavy sticker shock; permit fees in some California cities have exceeded $100,000. The following table presents the fees for a 2,000 square foot single family detached residence of medium quality. Some fees, such as building permit, are based on cost per square foot and may have two or three different cost bases, depending upon the building official's perception of the quality. Other fees, such as the school fee, are usually based upon the square footage; or may be a flat fee, such as the wastewater or park fees. The water fee is usually based upon meter size, although there is often one fee for the meter and another for resource development or storage.

If the sewer treatment plant is at capacity, or water availability exhausted, it doesn't matter what the fee is, you will not be able to obtain a permit. You will need to obtain school fee information from the local school district and, most likely, pay them directly. They will issue a receipt which you must present to the building official before he will issue your permit.

## PERMIT FEES FOR A SINGLE FAMILY RESIDENCE
## IN
## PETALUMA, CALIFORNIA

| | |
|---|---|
| Grading Permit | $ 50 |
| Building Division Plans Review | 2,711 |
| Engineering Review | 407 |
| Fire Department Review | 678 |
| Earthquake Motion | 18 |
| Energy | 678 |
| Plans Microfilming | 12 |
| Seismic Mapping | 8 |
| Building Permit | 2,711 |
| Plumbing Permit | 118 |
| Electrical Permit | 94 |
| Mechanical Permit | 46 |
| Temporary Utilities | 88 |
| City Facilities Impact | 5,399 |
| Open Space Acquisition | 379 |
| Park Land Acquisition | 1,616 |
| Park Development Impact | 5,212 |
| Traffic Impact | 18,978 |
| Wastewater Capacity | 7,166 |
| Water Capacity | 3,488 |
| Storm Drain Impact | 375 |
| Affordable Housing | 9,022 |
| School Fees | 4,034 |
| Total Permit Fees | $53,277 |

83

# NEGOTIATING A PLANS CONTRACT

| DO I NEED HELP? | |
|---|---|
| Big Project – it depends | Small Project – probably not |

When entering a contract for planning services you must have a clear understanding of your goal. You need to know what you need; and just as importantly, what you don't need. If your project is to redo the shower in your master bathroom, you don't need a site plan, details of your kitchen or other peripheral information. If you plan to add a room, you not only need a site plan, but you may need a soils test, drainage plan and even a drainage study, depending upon your jurisdiction. Even if not strictly relevant or seemingly necessary, many building and planning departments require information beyond common sense. Check with your local building department. You likely will have no choice but to go along with whatever they require.

Planning services may be generally divided into five components:

> Feasibility
> Entitlements
> Construction Documents
> Permit application and issuance
> Construction Oversight

The planning services contract may include all or only some of the components. The best party for compliance or quality control may not be the best choice for contract management or permit processing, for instance.

design & planning

Construction documents can be subdivided into drawings and specifications. Construction oversight can be subdivided into compliance, quality control, and contract management which itself can be subdivided into payment requests and change orders.

Construction drawings are just what the name implies – the actual drawings showing "what" is to be built; specifications are the written instructions on "how" the project is to be built. For instance, the plans may show a door; the specifications will name the type of door, what it is made of, the manufacturer, the finish and the hardware. Think of the plans as the playing field and the specifications as the rulebook.

85

Plans can vary widely (and wildly) in their comprehensiveness and the amount of detail. Various levels of thoroughness may be appropriate for different situations. For instance, new cabinets and tile in a hallway bathroom may not even need a plan, while a total reconfiguration and room extension of your kitchen may need extensive drawings, especially if structural issues are involved.

A builder working for himself may be comfortable with very cursory plans providing just a general outline of what is to be done; he is experienced and will be performing the work himself. You, on the other hand, are likely not an experienced builder (although I hope that experienced builders read this book as well) and probably will be relying upon your plans to obtain bids and to guide the builder you choose through the building process. Therefore you need good, thorough information leaving very little to interpretation or chance. The more information, the less probability of error or misunderstanding – both of which will cost you money and grief. The trick is to balance efficiency and expense with sufficient information. Do not get carried away – after all, as we noted earlier, you are not building a nuclear power plant – but be thorough enough to be clear.

There are many standard procedures in building that do not necessarily need a drawing to explain; often a note will suffice. The scope of the plans you order will depend in large part upon how you intend to use them – and upon the requirements of your local building department.

When the project is a remodeling project you will need "as built" drawings. These depict the conditions as they exist prior to start of construction.[17] Greater or lesser amounts of information may be appropriate. Again, your local building official can provide guidance.

Spend time discussing the scope of your plans requirements with your plans provider (whether it be an architect, draftsman or design/builder). Try to be clear on what you think you need; don't be afraid to ask questions or to challenge your plans provider. Don't be embarrassed by what you think you do not know – it doesn't matter. Be sure to understand the purpose of each proposed component in the planning package. A good consultant will understand your needs, the amount of documentation needed (both for approvals and for construction) and will respect your budget.

## Contracting with an Architect

An architect who is a member of the American Institute of Architects (AIA) will generally use a standard contract form published by the AIA. There are a number of AIA forms used for residential work. The forms and their descriptions can be found on the AIA website: http://www.aia.org/contractdocs/AIAS076745).

---

[17] "As built drawings" also refers to a set of project drawings annotated during the course of construction to indicate any changes in the construction as "actually" built, versus how the plans depicted "to be" built. As built differences do not necessarily imply errors or non-compliant solutions, but are often the result of differing site conditions, available materials or alternate ways of doing a thing approved by the architect. They are a record for use in future maintenance or renovation of a building.

---

### DO I NEED A LAWYER?

Big Project – it depends          Small Project – not if you're careful

---

AIA contracts are widely used and accepted.  Some professionals (me included) believe they are unduly slanted towards the architect, but generally the documents are considered thorough and fair.  The AIA has been publishing and refining these documents for over 100 years.

You may use an AIA document even if you are not contracting services with an AIA architect, however they are copyrighted and you may not use them without consent.  Contract forms may be purchased online directly from the AIA.[18]

**87**

Although these are commonly used forms, don't let them intimidate you.  Feel free to challenge any clause in any contract (not just AIA contracts) you are considering signing.  Any pre-printed contract may be modified by attaching an addendum signed by both parties or interlineation[19].  If you are uncomfortable with any term or condition ask to have it modified.  In most cases there will be a solution agreeable to both parties.  This will be the first test of your relationship with your architect, planner or designer.  If, at this early stage, you find them intransigent or difficult to work with, do not assume it will get better.  This might be a clue that you should continue your search.

---

[18] AIA forms may be viewed online at www.topfloorstore.com; forms may also be purchased or leased from this site.

[19] Interlineation is the inserting handwritten changes to the language, or the lining out the language as printed.  Interlineations must be initialed by both parties to be valid.

> ### WARNING
>
> A contract means only – and exactly – what the words ***actually*** say.  If you do not like what the words say, ask for a change.  If the opposite party tries to explain what it "really" means, ask him or her to change the language to say just that.  If they say they cannot do so, DON'T SIGN.  That means they don't believe what they are trying to convince *you* to believe.  Remember, the words mean only what they say, never anything else.  The willingness of the opposite party to agree to contract language that protects you – if it is fair – is the first test for reliability in your choice of an architect or builder.

**88**

Generally speaking you probably do not need a lawyer to review an AIA contract.  A better review would be by a contractor to address the completeness and appropriateness of the scope of work being defined and included.  A good contractor will be able to point out important omissions, or excess baggage (which your architect may dispute; hopefully, since I cannot be there for you, this book will give you guidance to sort out these types of conflicting viewpoints).

If your project is very large, involving design fees and construction costs which are significant, remember this advice:  an attorney consulted *before* the problem is ALWAYS cheaper than the attorney consulted *after* the problem.  Use an attorney who specializes in construction law.

## CONTRACT FUNDAMENTALS

A contract is a meeting of the minds between two parties. Generally one party agrees to perform a service or provide goods, and the second party agrees to pay for the service or goods, usually with money although payment may be made in services or goods also.

A contract needs to set forth in detail what is to be provided by the first party, for instance architectural services. However, a contract stating merely "architectural services" as the product would be vague, non-informative and ripe for dispute. A well written contract will spell out in detail what is to be provided: for instance, to create and provide a site plan, grading plan, floor plans, sections, elevations, etc., for a three bedroom, two bath house of approximately 2,000 square feet. Furthermore it should go into some level of detail about what is to be included in each of the components. For instance, the floor plans should include dimensions, door sizes, room names, window locations and sizes, cabinet locations, plumbing locations, and any other information you believe is needed to create a complete plan. The purpose for which it is to be used may also be stated – such as 80% complete for preliminary estimates; or construction ready.

There may also be general requirements, such as one stating that the architect guarantees plans review approval by the building division and that he will make all needed revisions to achieve same without additional charges. Another important clause will be ownership of the drawings. Usually the architect will want to retain ownership, whereas it is in the client's interest that he or she obtain ownership. Then the question becomes, at what point do you gain ownership.

The contract needs to set forth how much is to be paid for the services rendered, and when payment is due.

89

---

### CONTRACT FUNDAMENTALS (cont.)

Any contract should define how payment is earned. Payments for services contracts are usually based upon a schedule which assigns values to the different tasks contracted for in the agreement. Payment may be due only upon completion of a task; or it may be due periodically, usually monthly, based upon percentage of completion. Larger dollar value agreements usually use the second method, while smaller dollar value agreements typically use the first.

Regardless of the payment method, it is important that one be defined and that you, as the client, understands what constitutes completion, or how to determine percentage completed.

A contract should also have provision for early termination (a condition that will often give rise to dispute over ownership of the drawings).

**90**

---

A services proposal from an architect will often include fees for his consultants: soils engineer, civil engineer, structural engineer, mechanical engineer, energy calculations and even landscaping design. During due diligence you may already have performed a soils investigation. Also, the need for specialty consultants will often depend in large part upon the size and nature of your contemplated project.

An architect may engage the consultants directly, in which case the cost is built into the architect's contract; or he may arrange to coordinate their work and have you contract with them directly. This arrangement may be less expensive, but then you are faced with entering multiple contracts, managing additional payments and even coordinating their services. I generally have no strong opinion one way or the other as long as the architect undertakes to coordinate services.

## Contracting with a Planner

Planners deal with uncertainties. Therefore they prefer to enter hourly rate contracts as opposed to fixed price. The key to managing a planning contract is close communication with the planner. Be sure you know when and how much time he or she is spending, or plans to spend, on a task, and what that task is. Be sure to understand how and why it is relevant. With open ended contracts it is very important that you stay closely involved and constantly monitor the time spent. Remember, you will be billed for every minute of time – including drive time and waiting time – that your planner spends or your project.

## Hiring an Expeditor

The task of an expeditor, unlike that of a designer, is usually more clearly defined, although the time to achieve that task is rarely knowable with any certainty. You may retain an expeditor, for instance, to negotiate with the plans reviewer whether special structural engineering is required, or whether the project can be approved using standards embedded in the code. While the goal is clear, as being able to know if and when it has been accomplished, the time to achieve it is uncertain.

Because of this uncertainty most agreements with expeditors are a simple one page document setting forth a task or tasks and an hourly billing rate. Be sure you know when the clock starts and stops – for instance driving time, prep time, etc. Many expeditors have variable rates based upon the task. Also be clear on charges for expenses – mileage, copies, etc. These types of contracts are generally terminable at will, regardless of whether the assigned task has been completed or not. Be sure that you are entitled to all work papers without further payment at the end of the assignment or in the event you terminate early.

---

### FIXED PRICE VERSUS HOURLY?

Hourly may save you money if all goes well, but you are retaining the risk. Fixed price shifts the risk to the service provider. The pricing of a fixed price contract reflects the provider's estimate of and acceptance of that risk. The risk pricing in planning contracts will tend to be very high do to the inherent uncertainty, hence they are often unit priced (by the hour). Likewise for design agreements.

Architectural services and construction pricing is more definable and the risk premium will be lower – sometimes quite low. Be wary of too low a price however. You do not want your service provider getting into trouble. The best rule? Just be fair.

---

## Contracting with a Designer

A contract agreement with a designer will almost always be simpler than one with any other professional on your team. Often these agreements are as short as one page. Also, design services are unique in that they tend not to have a clearly defined end. Be careful, for although the work tends to be informal, remember that your designer will be billing for his or her time, even if it only seems to be conversations or otherwise lacking visible work product. This is legitimate because the designer has to mentally "conceive" what you want before actually making drawings. Depending upon how well you convey your ideas, and how efficient your decision making is, this can take some time.

## Contracting with a Draftsman

A draftsman is a technician. This is a key difference from an architect, who is part designer, planner, engineer, draftsman and project manager. A draftsman does one thing – draw plans. Some do it very well; others, well, not so good. Be careful with draftsmen; they are often self-taught and may lack up-to-date or in depth building code knowledge. Unlike an architect, they are not licensed and are not subject to professional oversight and accountability and may not carry E&O insurance (see the next page). A set of plans which fails to pass plans review or leaves out vital information will cost you far more in the long run than the money you thought you saved. If all the necessary information for what is to be built, and how, is not included in the plans you will quickly learn more than you ever wanted to know about change orders. If it is not in the plans, or presented incorrectly, you generally cannot expect that your contractor "should have known" what was intended. (As a short aside – yes, sometimes you can; but often you cannot. Besides, you really don't want to go down that road.)

## Contracting with an Engineer

If you have entered a contract with an architect, any needed engineering services are likely included. In general an engineering contract is similar to an architectural contract, although it is usually more limited in nature – addressing only certain technical aspects of the project.

A **structural engineer** deals only with the engineering aspects of assembling the foundation and frame of a building. He is the guy who does the calculations on footing and beam sizes, nailing patterns, connection details and the like. He considers wind loads (how hard the wind is likely to blow against the side of a building, and how strong the building must be to resist that load), snow load, seismic loads and soils bearing capacity. For soils bearing, he will rely upon a soils investigation report prepared by the geotechnical engineer.

You must be clear in your contract documents who is responsible for the soils testing. (It is usually you unless you specifically agree otherwise with either your architect or structural engineer.)

The **civil engineer** is responsible for the grading and drainage plan. In larger projects he will design the roads, water lines, sewers and storm drains.

The **electrical, mechanical and plumbing engineers** will design those specific requirements. Often one engineer will do all three, but not always. Smaller projects rarely develop separate MEP plans, but it is wise to engage professionals to design mechanical and electrical systems on larger projects.

**94**

Another professional service usually needed now is the **energy consultant**. The energy consultant will calculate heat gain or loss through windows, walls, etc. There will be energy standards that must be complied with and this consultant will determine if the design does so. It is wise to have the energy consultant involved early, especially in extreme climates. It would be a shame to spend thousands of dollars, and get all excited about a dramatic, window intensive design solution, and run into energy loss issues that could have been identified and resolved early in the process. If you have a mechanical engineer, the energy consultant may logically be included in his contract – but don't assume it is. Specify so if that is your desire.

## Consultants' Insurance

Regardless of the professional you retain to create your construction documents, be certain that they maintain a policy of errors and omissions insurance (E&O).[20] E&O is provides professional services providers defense and damages coverage in the event their work product is adjudged defective and themselves liable to their client for monetary damages. You may ask your

---

[20] Also known as professional liability insurance or professional indemnity insurance.

expeditor or planning consultant for E&O, but they are less likely to carry such coverage. A licensed architect will absolutely carry E&O (or don't hire him or her). A designer or interior decorator is very unlikely to carry E&O.

## Contracting with a Design/Builder

Contracting with a design/builder is a completely different animal. With design/build you are contracting not just for design and architectural services, but for the actual construction of your project. See page 124 for a complete discussion of design/build.

95

**96**

---

## DESIGN and PLANNING CONTRACTS CHECKLIST

The following are tasks which may be included in a design services agreement and the scope of work typically included in each task:

- Feasibility Review
  - Zoning code review
  - Preliminary environmental assessment
  - Utilities availability
  - Design guidelines and restrictions

- Design Development
  - Site visit
  - Research design guidelines and restrictions
  - Multiple client meetings (a limit is usually established)
  - Preliminary sketches, both plan view and exterior elevations
  - Optional
    - Rendered floorplan
    - Elevation renderings

- Entitlements
  - Identification of issues
  - Meetings with city planners
  - Meetings with other public and private officials
  - Consultant reports
    - Drainage
    - Environmental
    - Archaeological
  - Prepare applications
  - Neighborhood meetings
  - Publish public notices
  - Presentation materials
  - Attend public hearings
  - Revisions

---

## DESIGN and PLANNING CONTRACTS CHECKLIST (cont.)

- Construction Documents
    - Architectural drawings (create a list of required drawings)
    - Structural review and drawings
    - Mechanical, Electrical and Plumbing (MEP) drawings
    - Site and grading plan
    - Landscaping plan
    - Specifications

- Competitive Bidding for the Work
    - Prepare bid documents
        - Invitation to Bid
        - Bid form
    - Pre-qualify bidders
    - Receive requests for information (RFPs)
    - Issue bid addenda in response to RFPs
    - Conduct bid opening
    - Bid review
    - Select winning bidder
        - Proposed price
        - Exclusions

- Negotiated Bidding
    - Does the consultant conduct the negotiation
    - What disclosures are required by contractor
    - Are there conflicts of interest

97

98

## DESIGN and PLANNING CONTRACTS CHECKLIST (cont.)

- Prepare Construction Contract
  - Recommend contract form
  - Draft terms of contract
  - Scope of Work
  - List of Drawings
  - Conditions for payment
  - Schedule of Values
  - Performance Schedule

- Construction Management
  - Subcontractor approval
  - Submittal and shop drawing review
  - Compliance inspections
  - Quality control inspections
  - Payment request review and approval
  - Change proposal review and recommendation
  - Change order preparation
  - Review and approval of As Built drawings

# CONTRACTORS & BIDDING

# CONTRACTORS

Most states in the United States require that any person or business performing construction services, as other than a payroll employee, be licensed. Most states issue licenses at the state level, although a few, such as Colorado, issue licenses at the municipal level. Licenses are issued in numerous categories from general building to specialties, such as electrical, plumbing or asbestos removal. To obtain a contracting license the candidate generally must meet minimum experience requirements, take and pass a knowledge test, pass a background check, post a bond and maintain liability and workers compensation insurance. In California alone there are over 295,000 licensed contractors, including 105,000 licensed general building contractors for a population of 38 million. There are more contractors than there are lawyers.

In this section we talk about contractors – the good and the bad. We discuss estimating and bidding your project and utilizing the MasterFormat system for organizing the work of a construction project. We spend time considering how to find and choose a good contractor; how to offer a project to bid; and how to understand the bids you receive. We look at the various options for managing your project – from fee basis contractor to owner-builder. We introduce you to industry standard billing and payment practices, including an important discussion of construction liens and how to protect yourself from financial liability.

103

# TYPES OF CONTRACTORS

## General Contractors

General contractors will contract directly with an owner and usually assemble teams of subcontractors to perform a project, in addition to those tasks which they perform with their own labor force. The general contractor is responsible for the performance of the subcontractors he employs. The "general"[21] will provide job site supervision, back office support (in the person of a project manager), power, sanitary facilities, trash receptacles and other general services for the project. He will set and direct the schedule. He will also be responsible for assembling, contracting with and paying the subcontractors.

The prime contractor will usually line up its team of subcontractors during the bid process. Just as several prime contractors may be bidding against one another for the project, many subcontractors may also be bidding for their specialty portions of the work. While the general contractors bid to only the owner, the sub-contractors will often provide their proposals to several or all of the prime bidders.

Public works bidding procedures usually require that the bidder's selected subcontractors be named in the bid proposal. Among other reasons this allows the contracting agency to see and pre-approve the members of the general contractor's team before awarding the contract. It is common practice, however, in private work for the winning general contractor to "buy out" his project after the award by continuing to solicit or negotiate prices with his vendors in an attempt to lower his costs. From the standpoint of the owner

104

---

[21] On large projects the general contractor is usually referred to as the "prime" contractor, and the subcontractors may have subcontractors of their own, known as "sub-tier".

there is not really any harm, provided the owner reserves the right to approve any subcontractor to be used on his project.

A typical bathroom or kitchen remodel will involve approximately eight different trades:

| | |
|---|---|
| Demolition | Countertops |
| Plumbing | Painting |
| Electrical | Finish Carpentry |
| Drywall | Ceramic Tile |

General contractors who specialize in this type of work may perform some or even all of the work with their own forces. Many jurisdictions require that plumbing and electrical tradesmen be licensed themselves, so the general contractor will need to employ qualifying tradesmen. Ask your contractor if your jurisdiction requires licensing of plumbers and electricians and, if so and he intends to perform that work with his own employees, have him provide verification that they have the appropriate licenses.

105

## Subcontractors

Most general contractors prefer to subcontract specialty trades. A subcontractor, also referred to as a "specialty contractor" does just that – specializes in a certain phase of work, such as plumbing, drywall or roofing, and is expert in that area to a greater degree than a general contractor usually is. A general contractor specializes in orchestrating the entire construction project, bringing together all the diverse requirements and many specialties needed to deliver the completed whole, and manages the process to success.

By entering a subcontract for a given area of the work, the general contractor has fixed his costs and transferred risk. The other reason general contractors like using specialty contractors is that they gain the expertise of a contractor who performs this type of work full time. His systems and his employees are more proficient at delivering the work, thus, as a rule, leading to better quality product and quicker delivery.

When constructing an entire house from the ground up the number of trades expands. A typical list for a new home might include over 25 trades and 100 or more different workers. Keeping track of all this activity is the duty of the general contractor and, more specifically, his on site superintendent and his project manager.

## 106   MORE TYPES OF CONTRACTORS

Contractors can be broadly categorized into commercial, residential, and engineering contractors. Commercial contractors specialize is buildings used for commerce – restaurants, offices, warehouses. Engineering contractors build roads, bridges and industrial plants. Residential builders specialize in homes and apartments. There are, of course, all sorts of permutations, sub-categories and overlaps.

Contractors also come in levels of sophistication – from "pickup truck" to giant multi-billion dollar corporations. With increasing levels of sophistication come increased capacity and capabilities. Capacity is simply the ability of a contractor to handle a certain amount of work, usually expressed in dollars. A company must have the expertise (capability) to perform work in order to achieve greater capacity. To have capability and capacity, a company must have assembled a team of managers, a skilled workforce, a stable of subcontractors, equipment, institutional knowledge and working capital.

Commercial and civil contractors usually have greater capacity than residential contractors; and exception being the large national homebuilders.

Residential building tends to have more of a local focus, with greater emphasis on the one-on-one relationship between the builder and the client.

As a homeowner you will be working with a residential contractor. There are various levels of residential contractors.

## Pickup Truck Contractors

A pickup contractor is a term usually applied to a single individual who often performs much of the work himself, lacks an office and has very little capacity. Literally, or figuratively, his office is the front seat of his pickup truck. While he may be very capable as an individual, he is not a company and lacks the organization or resources to undertake significant projects. His paperwork is often poor.

Pickup truck contractors may offer what appears to be better pricing, but it comes at significant risk. Those risks include lack of liability or workers compensation insurance, workers that are often not employees or are undocumented, workers who lack training, lack of a safety plan and enforcement (or even knowledge) of safety rules and procedures, failure to provide sanitary facilities, and a willingness to cut corners to make up for low pricing. Supervision may be a problem; working cash is nearly always a problem,

That said, many successful contractors started as pickup truck contractors and, because of their dedication, hard work and desire to improve, quickly grew to become legitimate businesses. Most remodeling contractors are small, very small, businesses; most generate only a million dollars or (much) less in annual revenues. Qualified Remodeler magazine publishes an annual list of the largest remodelers in the country. The largest full service home remodeling company in the country has only $35,000,000 in annual sales (compared with the largest new homebuilder by revenues – Pulte Homes – with over $4 billion in total sales). Compared with production homebuilding, custom home building and remodeling is very fragmented and conducted by hundreds of local builders performing only a few jobs each year.

There are very good builders in every local market in the country; finding a good builder will not be a problem if you are willing to do your homework. Most homebuilders and remodelers began as tradesmen, usually as a carpenter, working on small custom home or remodeling projects because they just plain liked to build. As they matured, the best of them became licensed contractors and began soliciting work on their own – pickup truck contractors – and those with good business sense began to put together the people and parts that make a company. Those who performed well found that their customers recommended them to friends, and their businesses grew. Typically the owners of these small businesses worked – and many still do – sixty or more hours every week, involved in every aspect of their projects and their businesses.

## Paper Contractors

This is a term used to describe contractors who subcontract all or most of the work of a project except supervision. Although it is often used derogatorily, I disagree that it is necessarily a bad thing. There is no objective, compelling reason why a worker employed directly by the contractor, as opposed to a subcontractor, will do better work. In fact, the opposite is often true – your general contractor might be forced to have his direct employees perform any number of different trades in order to keep them busy, while a tradesperson working for a subcontractor will be regularly employed only at his special trade. Think about it – a worker or contractor specializing and working constantly in one area will – almost by definition – be better and more skilled at that trade than one who only works at it part of the time.

Your goal is to have the best workers, by whomever they are employed.

The real downside to you, as the buyer of services, is that each subcontractor will have his own overhead and profit markup. Thus, the more subcontractors, the more line items with subcontractor markups are priced into the contract. On the other hand, if your prime contractor is able to lay off the risk to a subcontractor he is generally willing to work for a lower margin than if he is assuming more of the risk by self performing greater amounts of work.

Also important is the length and standing of the relationships your contractor has with his subcontractors.

**109**

## Owner Builder

Unless you could write this book yourself, **THINK TWICE!** And even then, it might not be a good idea.

If you choose to be a self builder you had better be prepared for all the challenges that come with the turf. These include: obtaining a building permit, liability insurance, finding and qualifying subcontractors, writing scopes of work, obtaining and analyzing bids, performing materials takeoffs, soliciting price quotes, purchasing and delivery of materials, shortages, storage, perhaps hiring and managing workers you might employ directly (which triggers workers compensation insurance, unemployment insurance and reports, payroll and withholding tax, quarterly and annual payroll tax returns, and payroll capital), preparing the project schedule, no-shows, arranging for dumpsters and trash removal, daily cleanup, sanitary facilities, safety kit, parking, daily supervision, plans clarifications and solutions, building inspections, possibly an OSHA[22] inspection, certificate of occupancy and at least

---

[22] Occupational Health and Safety Administration. Workers compensation rates will tell you something about the risk of accidents on home projects. Work comp rates are set by category

a dozen more minor and major tasks that I haven't mentioned, depending upon the project, including disputes and dispute resolution.

It will be you who will deal directly with everything. You will have no-one to help you; everyone you are dealing with will be first and foremost looking out for their self-interest, not yours. Direct hire workers cannot be left without supervision. The level of sophistication can vary widely among the trades contractors, and even within the trades. Electricians and heating, ventilation and air conditioning (HVAC) contractors are generally more sophisticated than drywall contractors, for instance, and the quality of performance and paperwork varies accordingly. Be sure you are ready for this before you attempt it yourself.

You yourself will have to determine if the work is properly executed, and if the quality is acceptable. Will you know when to challenge it? How will you handle it when the challenged worker or contractor disputes your call? Are you sure of your judgment, or is he right? Is what he telling you valid, or is it smoke?

Are you prepared to purchase the proper insurance for your project? Is it economical for you to do so? You have no experience rating module (based on your lack of a track record as a contractor), so your liability policy is going to bill at the highest rate.

Do you have the time? If you are working a regular job, the answer is simple: NO, you do not. Are you physically able to meet the demands of being on your feet most of the day at a jobsite and then coming home at night to do paperwork?

---

and trade. Rough carpentry on commercial jobs typically has a work comp rate of about 12%; the rate on single family detached houses is usually in the 30% range. As rates are a reflection of risk, it is clear that you are two and a half times more likely to have an accident on a project at your home than a commercial contractor is on his jobsite.

Even a simple project like a bathroom remodel can soon become overwhelming if you lack experience in construction management. Enthusiasm can quickly wear thin.

## FINDING A BUILDER

Go online and google "homebuilder", "custom homebuilder", "remodeling contractor" and similar terms. You will get lots of hits. Personally, I believe a website tells a lot about the quality of a business. If it is well organized and informative, that is often a clue about how the business perceives itself and how well they perform – the quality of their work. In my mind, if a business fails to care about how they present themselves – how they appear to their potential customers – I have to wonder how much they care about the work they produce.

I always look first at the "About Us" tab. I want to see who I will be dealing with; who owns the company, what they look like and what they have to say. I want to see personal input; relevant, not generic. Most successful builders will tell you about themselves – after all, they should be proud of themselves – and have galleries of completed projects and testimonials from satisfied clients.

Referrals from friends or neighbors are also a great source. If you know anyone who has built a home or remodeled, ask them if they recommend their builder; or if they know anyone who might. Do not necessarily take a recommendation at face value; your project may be more complex, or the person making the recommendation may not be qualified to render an informed opinion. Ask what particular things their builder did that they liked, and what they did not like.

Keeping your eyes open for building projects as you are out and about is another good way to not only find builders, to also to see what they are building.

There are also online prospecting services, such a Service Magic and HomeAdvisor.com which run multiple websites to prospect for leads which they then sell to independent contractors who pay a fee to subscribe to the service. Referrals by these, and similar, lead generators are not a recommendation of the contractor; these companies do not pre-qualify the contractors – not even to the point of verifying that they are contractors. The same lead is handed out to multiple buyers, and the companies who buy them compete almost solely on price. Bluntly, this is a lazy, uniformed and careless way to select a contractor.

Your best choice for a builder is a company with strong local roots and a strong portfolio of completed projects. Such companies will have experienced managers and tested relationships with subcontractors, are conscious of their reputations and dedicated to their craft.

Many of the selection techniques discussed in the section of this book on choosing a design professional are applicable to choosing a contractor.

## Trade Organizations

There are a number of organizations for residential builders and remodelers. Top quality builders are interested in improving how they perform. Belonging to trade and peer organizations is an excellent way to keep up with latest trends and technologies and is an excellent indicator of the dedication and interest a builder has in his chosen profession.

The largest and most prominent of these organizations is the National Association of Homebuilders. Founded in 1942, the NAHB has over 140,000 individual and corporate members and plays a major role in housing policy, research and technical advancement in the United States and Canada. There are over 800 local chapters nationwide. The annual NAHB convention and trade show is the fifth largest trade show in the nation.

Many types of organizations belong to the NAHB, from giant materials manufacturers and national, publicly traded homebuilding corporations, to small, local homebuilders. In fact, the NAHB has a special organization called the 20 Clubs which brings similar type builders from across the nation together in groups of twenty to share their experience (and experiences) with each other. Many small homebuilders are actually quite prominent in the NAHB. Find the NAHB online at www.nahb.org.

**113**

NARI is the National Association of the Remodeling Industry. NARI's stated goal is "to advance and promote the remodeling industry's professionalism, product and vital public purpose." To further its goals, NARI conducts continuing education seminars for its members and encourages sharing of experiences and information. NARI has also created a Code of Ethics for the remodeling industry which each of its members pledges to abide with. The NARI website has a wealth of information for anyone contemplating a remodeling project on their home. Go to www.nari.org.

The National Kitchen and Bath Association (NKBA) is an organization of 50,000 members in 72 local chapters throughout the United States and hosts the Kitchen and Bath Industry show, also one of the largest annual trade shows in the country. The NKBA acts as a clearing house for trade information, encourages improvements in materials and design and provides ongoing education for its members.

The United States Green Building Council is a membership organization which provides over 324 hours of classroom training in green building theory and techniques as well as a library of hundreds of timely and pertinent articles.

The USGBC also sponsors the LEED green building program in the United States.

---

## WHAT IS LEED?

LEED (Leadership in Energy and Environmental Design) is a voluntary, consensus-based, market-driven program that provides third-party verification of green buildings. From individual buildings and homes, to entire neighborhoods and communities, LEED is transforming the way built environments are designed, constructed, and operated. Comprehensive and flexible, LEED addresses the entire lifecycle of a building.

Participation in the voluntary LEED process demonstrates leadership, innovation, environmental stewardship and social responsibility. LEED provides building owners and operators the tools they need to immediately impact their building's performance and bottom line, while providing healthy indoor spaces for a building's occupants.

LEED projects have been successfully established in 135 countries.

---

## Publications

There are a number of publications geared toward homebuilding and remodeling professionals. While some, such as Builder magazine, are aimed at larger, corporate builders, others may be of interest to homeowners contemplating undertaking their own project. These include Qualified Remodeler and Remodeling magazines. Both have online archives which are both interesting and helpful. Fine Homebuilding and Custom Home magazines are geared towards the craft of building.

## HOUSING MILESTONES

| | |
|---|---|
| 3400 BC | Plywood is invented by the ancient Mesopotamians. Modern plywood is invented in the mid-1800's by Immanuel Nobel, father of Alfred Nobel |
| 1894 | The earliest form of drywall was invented |
| 1908 | Sears Roebuck offers its first "Modern" kit houses through its catalog for $650. Sears sold over 70,000 catalog homes until discontinuing them in 1940 |
| 1944 | 142,000 new homes completed in the United States |
| | The GI Bill is signed into law creating the first VA mortgage and unleashing the post WWII housing boom |
| 1947 | 1.2 million new homes completed in the United States |
| 1957 | Baby boom peaks at 4.3 million births |
| 1959 | Average new home price across the United States is between $13 - $20,000 |
| 1962 | President Kennedy signs executive order banning housing discrimination. |
| 1965 | HUD, the federal Department of Housing and Urban Development, is created |

115

HOUSING MILESTONES (cont.)

| | |
|---|---|
| 1968 | The federal Fair Housing Act is enacted |
| 1987 | The 100 millionth house in the United States is completed |
| 1989 | Asbestos banned in residential construction |
| 2004 | Housing ownership in the United States reaches 69% of all households, an all time high |
| 2006 | The great housing bust begins |
| 2007 | Average house price in the United States peaks at $238,000 |

116

## CHOOSING A BUILDER

Once you have narrowed your search to several builders who look promising, it is time to begin your due diligence. Your architect will have had experience with a number of builders. Hopefully he will steer you away from any bad builders and recommend qualified candidates for you to consider.

You will, of course, want to meet and interview builders. This is going to be a multi-month relationship involving money and your life. You must like, trust and be comfortable with the person with whom you are dealing.

## Personality

Initially you will be testing them for compatibility and congeniality. While Joe Builder may come with superior credentials for performance and craftsmanship, you may find that you just aren't that comfortable with him one on one; or even that you just plain don't like him. Next.

Make sure your candidate is a good listener; however, you also want someone who will tell you what you need to hear. If you expect executive presence on your job every day, say so. Make sure they are prepared to accommodate you. If you anticipate needing a lot of hand-holding, make that clear. On the other hand, if you want to go to Europe for six months and come home to a finished job, make sure you select someone whom you trust to make solid decisions for you. And be sure you are willing to accept those decisions.

Above all, be realistic in your expectations and communicate them while interviewing potential candidates. Remember, they are also interviewing you. The strength of the relationship is also very important to them; they know how important it is to a successful job – and to their bottom line. Be honest and be clear.

## Attitude

If you interview a contractor and he bad mouths architects, or complains about how he can't get good help, or how hard the building inspector is to work with, he has raised a red flag. Dig deeper.

Remember that this is not a romance, it is a business relationship. You don't want surprises, drama or excitement. Someone who has been through the drill before will reduce the surprises and smooth the process. Look for someone who is successful. (Hint – a giant pickup truck is not an indicator of success.) Ask how many projects, and what type, his company completed last

117

year and the year before. Compare it to how many he has going or in the pipeline now. Growth is good; too much growth too fast could be at your expense.

## A Company or an Individual?

Is the candidate you are interviewing an individual, or is he the head or an organization? If your project is small, an individual may be the perfect solution. You will keep costs down, and if he is not too busy, you should receive lots of personal attention. He may even do much of the work himself.

**118**

But if your project is bigger, you probably need an organization. A complex project requires scheduling, purchasing, submittals and shop drawings, posting accounts, paying the bills and documentation as well as daily on-site supervision. Be sure that the capacity of your contractor matches the complexity of your project.

## References

Get references and contact them – homeowners, subcontractors, suppliers and architects. Ask subcontractors how organized your candidate is; do his jobs run smoothly. Were they treated fairly; were they asked to perform extra work without compensation (bad)? Ask subs and suppliers if payment is timely. Go to the building department and check the permit files. See what other jobs your potential builder has done that are not on his list of references. Contact them to see what they have to say. Also, try to gauge what you are hearing by who you are hearing it from. If the source seems unreliable, the information might well be unreliable also. Don't forget that there are two sides to every story.

Absolutely visit one or more of his current, ongoing jobs. Take a good look around. Is it clean; are there personnel at work; is there a job site office; is there a dumpster; is there a portable toilet; is the superintendent there; are safety rails in place? Ask questions about how long they've been under construction. Does the answer seem too long for the amount of work in place? Ask how the work is going; have them point out some of the highlights of the job. Look to see if the permit is visibly displayed. Do they have a project sign up? Is it firmly attached, level and clean? Is there loud music playing? Where are the workers' vehicles parked; is there mud in the street?

## Liens and Disputes

An awkward but important question is this: have you ever had to file a lien to get paid? More than once? Have them describe the circumstances and how it was resolved. You don't want someone who gets into money disputes. (By the way, one way to avoid this is to make sure the contract is for enough money to do the job.) A corollary is to ask if they have ever been sued by a vendor for payment.

A related question is whether he has ever been involved in disputes. We all have disagreements, but it's how we solve them that tells. Ask you candidate if he has ever been in a lawsuit or arbitration with a client. Don't assume he is the bad guy; some clients are impossible. Get his side of the story. Was it a dispute over money, change orders, quality or some misunderstanding due to poor contract documents? Is he bitter or philosophical? Ask him what he would have done differently in retrospect. How long ago was his last dispute? Of related interest is if he has been in disputes with subcontractors or suppliers. One or two disputes with subcontractors over the years can happen; disputes with clients are of more concern. There is no hard and fast rule here. Ask the questions and then you'll have to make the call.

**119**

## Financial Strength

The last thing you want is for your contractor to go broke. There are also stages before he goes broke that you want to avoid. Awkward though it may be, you have to ask questions about your potential builder's financial strength.

Construction work is done on the come, as it were. While contractors like to get advances or deposits, it is bad policy – both for you and, potentially, for him. You never want to pay for anything that has not been built or delivered to the site. It's just too easy for the money to disappear.

**120**

If you must give a deposit, use a letter of credit. If the supplier (or your contractor) lacks sufficient working capital to support his business for 30 – 60 days, they are probably not the right choice.

---

### LOST MONEY

Years ago I was building an agricultural inspection building for the State of Hawaii. Central to the facility was an irradiation chamber used to sterilize fruit prior to shipping to the Mainland in order to prevent the spread of fruit flies. As you might imagine, an irradiation chamber is a special order item, and at the time was only available with a long lead time from a long-standing company on the east coast. Naturally the company wasn't prepared to manufacture the chamber to our specs and ship it across the continent and the Pacific Ocean and trust that we'd send a check. So they asked for a substantial deposit. Which, despite misgivings, we sent.

Well, sure enough, the company took our money and promptly went broke. No chamber, no money, no profit. The moral: keep your money until you receive the goods.

---

## WHAT TO KNOW ABOUT YOUR CONTRACTOR

- Check for a valid and currently active contractor's license. This can usually be done online by going to the state regulatory board's website. In states which license at the local level, check with the building department in your city.

- Check with the licensing authority for disciplinary actions or complaints.

- Check with the Better Business Bureau for complaints and to obtain the company's BBB rating. Read any actual complaints and how the company responded.

- Check Angie's List.

- Confirm that the company has liability and workers compensation insurance.

- Does the company belong to trade organizations such as NARI or NAHB.

- Is, or has, the company been involved in any litigation. What was the outcome; what's his side of the story.

- How long has he been in business under this name? What was his previous business, if any?

- Has he ever declared bankruptcy; ever not finished a project?

- How many projects similar to mine has he completed? How recently?

121

122

## MORE TO KNOW ABOUT YOUR CONTRACTOR

- How many projects similar to mine have you completed? How recently?

- Ask for referrals and <u>contact</u> those referrals. Try to get a list of all his recent projects and contact them, whether he provides them as references or not. Remember, people only provide good references, never bad ones.

- Who will be supervising my work and what is their experience? How much time will that person spend on my jobsite?

- Which work do you perform with your own forces? Why?

- What criteria do you use to select your subcontractors? Who are some of your preferred subcontractors (this is part of their competitive advantage; you may find them reluctant to hand up their best vendors right off the bat.)

- What's the local building department like to work with (this can give you insight into their professional attitude).

- Show him your plans. Is he complimentary, derogatory; or does he have insightful, constructive comments?

- What contract type does he like?

- How often do you bill? How soon is payment due? (This will give a clue to the contractor's financial strength. A builder who bills weekly and wants paid immediately likely has cash flow issues.

## INTERVIEWING REFERRERS

These are questions to ask those who have referred or used a particular builder:

- Was the contract clear and fair

- Was the work delivered on time

- Was the work pursued on a daily basis, or were there days when no work was pursued

- Was there a supervisor on site at all times; if not, was he there as needed

- Did the supervisor answer his phone every time

- Were the workers and staff of the builder courteous and responsive

- Was the jobsite kept clean without having to ask; was there adequate dust protection provided

- Did the builder complain about changes

- Was the builder fair when pricing change orders

- Were billings front loaded

- Were lien waivers delivered without having to ask for them

- Were punchlist items performed promptly

- Did the builder provide a written warranty

- Was the builder adequately funded, or did he constantly need money

- Were all the bills paid and in a timely manner

- Would you work with this builder again

123

# DESIGN BUILD

Design/build construction contractors roll up preliminary planning, design, working drawings and construction under one roof. A design/build contractor will take you from idea to move-in with one stop. There are advantages to design/build and there are disadvantages.

The greatest advantage is that you have reduced the project to one relationship – one person (or entity) to deal with. There cannot be any finger pointing or unexpected costs for planning or design errors or omissions. The disadvantage, of course, is that you sacrifice competitive bidding for this convenience and assurance. You need to ask yourself if the convenience and transfer of "gaps" risk to the design/builder offsets any potential savings you might (or might not) gain by competitive bidding. ("Gaps" are those points of transition from one provider to another – from plans to building, for instance. A gap happens when the responsibility for the transition or "connects" between the two providers is not specifically assigned to either one. An example of an architect-builder gap would be the applying for and obtaining the building permit.)

Smaller projects are ideal for design/builders – bathroom and kitchen remodels, room additions and similar small projects where the extra layers of expense in the traditional approach quickly add up.

For larger projects – a new home from the ground up – the traditional approach of having the house designed and drawn by an architect may be the best choice, especially if you are interested in creating an architectural statement as well as building a new home. Different contractors often have very different ideas regarding costs or their willingness to accept risk (as reflected in their pricing) on a particular project. The differences in pricing on larger projects – half a million dollars or more – can be worth the extra effort of the traditional process.

124

Design/builders advance two powerful arguments. First, since they are designing *and* building the project, they have accepted responsibility for the completeness of the plans. In the traditional method, if there is an error or omission in the plans, the builder gets to submit a change order to cover the new or extra costs he incurs. This is because the builder accepts only the limited responsibility of performing the work as set forth in the plans – as actually drawn – not as they perhaps "should" have been drawn. Who pays? You do. By accepting the combined responsibility, the design/builder is obligated to solve the problem without involving you because there is no "gap" in responsibility.

The second advantage argued by design/builders is the organic budgeting process. Since the design/builder is both the designer of the work, and the estimator, he can determine while the design is ongoing how much the project will cost to build. That is, early in the game.

**125**

Therefore, if you are upfront with your design/builder about what your budget is, he can design to your budget. If you are like most clients I have had, your dreams and your budget are, to greater or lesser degree, not in alignment. Imagine a balance scale. The left hand side is weighed down with all the things that you want, the weight of which lifts the right hand side. The right hand side is how much your project is going to cost. Equilibrium is your budget. If your project is out of equilibrium, you costs are out of alignment with your budget and your project will or cannot get completed.

So what the design/builder does is work with you to design a project which is in equilibrium. This can be accomplished in one of two ways – either you increase your budget, or you modify your wishes.

The design/builder is constantly inputting costs as the design is being developed. He is able to keep you informed of the cost implication of every design decision *as* it is being considered, and before the expense of putting it into bid document form.

**126**

You are able to rely upon the design/builder's cost input – and this is critical – because he has committed to execute the work for the amount of the budget developed during the design process, as opposed to an architect or designer who accepted no risk of guaranteeing construction costs. This commitment must be a part of any design/build agreement, or you have lost the inherent value of design/build.

Be clear on the level of experience of the designer and plans preparer your design/builder assigns to your project. Be sure that their experience level is up to your project. If your project is a kitchen re-do, a kitchen designer using 20/20 kitchen design software is probably well up to the task. If your project is a 10,000 square foot house on a steep slope, you will need a highly qualified architect. Some design/builders have architects on staff; others work closely with outside architects who work through the design/builder.

A design/build contract may be in one or two parts. A two part design/build agreement separates the conceptual design and budgeting from the working drawings and construction. A preliminary agreement will be signed between you and the design/builder which will provide that he works with you to create a design and budget for a certain improvement described in the agreement. This is usually a simple one or two page document. It will limit the number of revisions (or design meetings) and set the price. It will not usually set the budget allowance, although it might (most homeowners prefer not to disclose their ultimate budget number, or may not even know for sure). It will have some standard language.

The second part of a design/build relationship will be the construction phase. This will include the preparation of working drawings in accordance with the design solution agreed to in the preliminary agreement. There may well be changes in the design as the working drawings are completed – sometimes significant changes. Be aware, that the further into the drawings you get, the greater the ripple effect of any change. Most design/builders (and architects, for that matter) will reserve the right to charge extra for any changes after a certain point. Nevertheless, if you really want the change, please make it. As I like to say, a change is always cheaper to make with a pencil and an eraser than with a nail puller or a jack hammer.

127

The build contract will set the price agreed upon for the work. It will be a complete construction contract except for completed working drawings, the completion of which is part of the contract deliverables. It should have a complete Scope of Work and set of Specifications attached when signed. The design sketches will be attached as an exhibit. The contract will have all the elements of any construction contract and, at this point in time, none of the conditions of the contract will be any different than any open bid or negotiated construction agreement, with the exception of the obligation to provide completed plans. The contract will also include language found in architectural services agreements as well as the construction specific language. The agreement should provide that the design/builder is to obtain the building permit.

### ARCHITECT vs. DESIGN/BUILD

An architect will not be directly involved in or responsible for the actual construction, so it is incumbent upon him or her to create a set of plans which provides all the information needed to complete the construction project as he or she and the owner intend.

Although the design/builder will be involved every step of the way in the construction, and it might seem that he would not need to detail every piece of information on the plans, he has an obligation to disclose to the homeowner his intentions. As well, he must provide the same information to the field that the architect conveys.

Therefore there should be little difference in the plans.

**128**

## CONSTRUCTION MANAGERS

An owner may elect to retain a construction manager to oversee and direct the entire process – from feasibility through planning, design, bidding and construction. Construction managers are often referred to as the owner's representative.[23] The best owner's reps are usually retired contractors or construction project managers. Ex-superintendents often lack the paperwork sophistication that is a big part of the value in having a good rep. Engineers and architects often get into owner's rep work, but – and this may just be my construction background talking – I believe they generally lack the hands on construction management and field experience to best represent an owner in the business of building, as opposed to the design and specifications aspects of building.

---

[23] Or "Owner's Rep".

Construction managers usually bill by the hour or day, but many are willing to enter fixed fee agreements for a project. Retaining services on an hourly basis allows you to pick and choose when you need them, but frugality may be misplaced. A good construction manager will save you many times his cost in job cost savings, greater efficiency, faster completion and (and this is a big one) peace of mind. Peace of mind (and your marriage) by itself is probably worth having a construction manager involved to some degree or other.

An owner's rep will have experience navigating the approvals bureaucracy; will manage the architect to assure that the plans are comprehensive, while not excessive; make sure the plans end up in alignment with your budget; and will prepare the bid package and solicit and qualify bidders. He or she will respond to requests for information, receive and open the bids and recommend an award. He or she will prepare the contract documents and exhibits. With the start of construction he or she will approve the contractor's schedule, conduct jobsite meetings, and assure the quality of the work. In all of this, the owner's representative advocates the interests of the homeowner – and only the interests of the homeowner. A good owner's representative delivers efficiency. cost savings and peace of mind to his or her client.

# BIDDING THE WORK

If your choice is to go the traditional method and have a set of plans prepared by an architect or drafting professional, then you will need to either put those plans out to bid or select a contractor with whom to negotiate a price. Negotiating a price with a contractor is similar in some ways to working with a design/builder, but without the plans development component. You will be working from a set of plans that you have already had prepared under separate agreement. However, and this is one of the benefits of negotiated contracts, the contractor with whom you are working may well suggest changes, either for the purpose of saving money, or for making construction easier (which should, almost by definition, save you money). The approach to the project becomes more collaborative. Depending upon the scope of these changes, the plans may need to be modified, which will most likely not be free. If the plans review has been completed, the changes must be re-submitted for review and additional approval.

If you elect to solicit competitive bids, you may do so in two ways — either by placing the plans in a plans room and letting all comers bid; or by inviting a selected group of contractors to bid. The first method is always used for public works and for much commercial work; the latter method is the norm for residential work. Residential plans will rarely be responded to in a plans room; commercial bidders believe private residential work to be too fickle and high maintenance.

You may conduct the bid yourself, or you may elect to have your architect conduct the bid. A third method is to retain a construction manager to conduct the bidding process.

Unless you are expert, or known in the construction community, contractors may be hesitant to respond to bid requests for one-off projects from unknown "amateurs". Bids solicited by homeowners are typically informally

130

requested, and without a prepared "Invitation to Bid" and professional bid documents set. This is a red flag to a contractor and he may be reluctant to participate. After all, it's a lot of work and expense to put a bid together and he wants some reasonable confidence that the project will go forward. Private home bids are well-known to come in over their owner's budget expectations and to go nowhere.

If contractor doesn't outright decline an invitation to bid directly from a homeowner, his bid may be more of a "ballpark" type bid. He won't put a lot of effort into it and his number will either be high – to cover himself – or artificially low assuming he can negotiate up to the right price. Subcontractors are even more reluctant. They have the same fears, and also know that early numbers are often renegotiated later. Many contractors will ask for proof of funding prior to committing to bid on a project. This is fair.

131

A good way to avoid these problems is to have the bid conducted by your architect or by a construction manager. Architects are usually more interested in designing, preparing drawings and even construction oversight than in preparing bid documents and conducting bids. On the other hand, this is what construction managers do.

## Bid Documents

A good set of bid documents will go a long way towards assuring good bid results. The best results are a clustered set of bids, with nobody dramatically higher or lower. If a bidder comes in significantly lower, be careful that he did not forget something. Absolutely, under no circumstances, try to take advantage of such a mistake. This will only come back to haunt you. That is as certain as the sun coming up tomorrow morning.

The bid documents consist of the Invitation to Bid, the Bid Form, the Plans and Specifications, any Addenda issued in response to questions by bidders, and, usually, the contract form.

## Invitation to Bid

The Invitation provides basic information: the owner's name, a brief statement of the scope of work, the project address, the architect's name and contact information, the construction manager's name and contact information, how and where to obtain plans and specs, the bid date and time, whether the bid is to be sealed.

**132**

## Bid Form

You will get better results if you require the bidders to submit their bids on a form which you provide to them. This way you control the information you receive and can be certain of comparing apples to apples. Allowing bidders to submit in their own format allows them the opportunity to modify the information being presented from what you are asking for (thus introducing the potential for "gaps"). You will have multiple bid presentations which you will be forced to check not only for compliance with the bid invitation and the construction documents, but also with each other. You must be sure that all bids are in alignment in order to determine who is the actual low bidder.

A Bid Form may be as simple as asking for a single lump sum number, or it may divide the work into a number of segments or options ("alternates"). It will often ask the bidder to commit to a number of days within which the work will be completed. It may also ask for options. Examples of a bid with options would be a base bid to build a house with options to construct a barn, or a swimming pool, or to provide landscaping. Alternate finish options may be asked for. Some bids end up being quite complex this way.

## Bid Opening & Review

Once the bids are received they must be opened and reviewed. Bid openings for public works are always public and the lowest fully compliant bidder is always awarded the project. Private projects may be opened publicly, but are more often opened privately by the conductor of the bid and the owner. Private bids, even those conducted using a bid format, often come in with options, exclusions or other conditions. Owners typically reserve the right to waive any irregularities in a bid proposal.

The owner and his advisors go over the bids and determine whom to award the contract to. The decision is usually based upon price, time of performance, past performance and reputation, and personal comfort level of the owner. The work load of the bidder may also be a factor. The results are almost never announced at the time of the bid opening. There is no inherent obligation to disclose the bid results to the bidders, although common courtesy dictates that you would.

Or no bidder may be awarded the project. If the bids all come in way over budget, it may be back to the drawing board; or the project may get scrapped altogether.[24] Or the low bidder, or a couple of bidders, may be asked to negotiate, which they may, or may not, be willing to do. Most contractors are willing to negotiate one on one, but are reluctant to do so if another bidder is involved. The reason for this is that the contractors will feel they are being played off against each other (which is most likely true), and will resent it. This is a poor way to potentially enter a relationship which could last for many

---

[24] Refer back to the design/build process discussed starting on page 50 as a method to avoid this outcome.

months. It is referred to a "bid shopping" and is considered by many to be ethically questionable. That doesn't mean it doesn't go on all the time.

With lump sum bids the contractor is normally not expected to disclose how he arrived at his bid estimate. In negotiated bids, the contractor will be expected to document how he arrives at his costs. This often entails obtaining and disclosing multiple (usually two or three) subcontractor or supplier bids for each line item in the project, detailed material and labor take-offs and other information the bidder may prefer not to disclose in detail.

In a contract negotiation there is no substitute for experience. A good construction manager or owner's rep can easily pay for himself – and more – in a contract price negotiation.

> Generally, building is like champagne – you get what you pay for.

## How Much Should a Contractor Make?

How much should your contractor make? How much does he make? In good times margins go up; in tough times they go down. That much we know for sure; after that there are no surefire rules. Contractors may present bids or state their markups in a number of different ways. Usually there will be a charge for overhead and then a charge for profit. First the total costs are added up to a subtotal. Then overhead is calculated as a percentage of that subtotal; the two are added together and then profit is figured as a percentage of that second subtotal. Other items may be added below the bottom line, such a performance bond fees, excise or sales taxes or liability insurance.

## Perception of Risk Affects Pricing

Directly affecting pricing is the contractor's perception of how risky the job is. This is a combination of subjective judgments: how good are the plans, how difficult is the site, how difficult is the building? How difficult is the client (yes, that is a consideration – in fact, a big one)? Also, will it be built in the rainy season, are there labor shortages, are the prices of materials in motion? Does he have a good superintendent available?

Other factors are how badly does he want, or need, this job; or what his perception is of the bidding strategy of competing bidders.

Every one of these factors is a consideration. If a contractor badly needs work, he will accept more risk for a lower premium; if he is flush, he will want more compensation in exchange for the risk you are asking him to accept.

**135**

## Lump sum

A lump sum (or fixed price) contract is by definition the most risky type of contract a builder can enter. In a lump sum contract the contractor agrees – guarantees – to deliver a defined amount of work for a price set in advance, regardless of how much, or how little, it costs him. If he figured it out right, he makes money – maybe even more than he anticipated. If he made an error in estimating, or fails to execute efficiently, the contract may well cost him more to complete than he will be paid.

While this may – may – seem to be a good thing for you, the buyer, it may also backfire. The positive is that you have fixed your budget; you have assurance as to how much money you are going to spend. If the bid was good, you're set. The problem is, if the bid is too low, especially way too low, the contractor could get into financial trouble and be unable to finish the job. This could lead to poor quality work, an abandoned project and even litigation. It could well cost you more in the long run, as well as delays and lots of stress.

What makes a good bid?  First, good construction documents; second good bid documents.  Then a clear understanding of the results.  While the rule of thumb is usually three bidders, I prefer five.  With three bidders, if all three are clustered within a few dollars of each other, you can have confidence that you have a good bid.  Go ahead and award the low bidder.

But what if one bidder is way low, one way high and the other right in the middle.  Which one is right?  Is the high bidder afraid of the job, not hungry, or ran out of time and just threw out a number that couldn't hurt himself?  Or does he know something the other guys don't?  And the low bidder – did he make a big mistake and miss something?  You don't want that problem.  So is the guy in the middle correct?  Hard to say.

**136**

Now if you have five bidders, there's a much better chance of getting a cluster.  Clusters are good when you are opening bids.

## Negotiated Bids

Any contractor would much rather negotiate his deal.  That way he's eliminated the competition and the dilemma of how tight he can cut it and still have a chance of making a profit.  Negotiated contracts can be cost-plus, fixed price or cost-plus not to exceed.

In cost-plus, the contractor earns either a percentage of the actual expenses or a flat fee.  Your contractor engages the vendors and runs the job. The contract amount is open-ended, being the actual costs of the project plus the fee.  You want a flat fee agreement.  With a percentage fee, the contractor has no incentive to hold costs down; in fact, his incentive is exactly the opposite.   In a fixed fee agreement, in the event of change orders, it is fair that the contractor be allowed a pre-set percentage of the extra work amount (or deduction).  There should also be an increase in the fee for delays beyond the control of the contractor. This gets tricky, and engaging the help of a experienced negotiator is probably well worth the expense.

In a fixed price negotiated contract, the results are exactly the same as a competitively bid contract – you just got there by negotiation instead of bidding. You have a set price which the contractor guarantees.

Cost-plus not to exceed is a hybrid. It functions as cost-plus, but the contractor has guaranteed the completion of all the specified work will not exceed some upper limit dollar amount. That way you cap your risk (also your savings), but in exchange for the added risk to him the contractor will want a higher fee. A variation is to share the cost savings 50/50 with your contractor, which gives him incentive. (Watch that he isn't "over" incentivized to the point of cutting corners.)

**137**

## Contingency

Every budget needs to have a contingency. This can be dealt with in a number of different ways. (What's the contingency for, you may ask your contractor. The answer: if he knew, it wouldn't be a contingency; it would be a named line item.) Sometimes the contingency is stated as single a line item, usually being a percentage of the total job costs amount; sometimes it is a percentage increase to each individual line item; sometimes different categories (or MasterFormat divisions) are given separate contingencies based upon the risk perception for each category. Tasks which are self-performed have more risk that tasks which are subcontracted out.

## Insurance

Insurance, usually considered as a fixed, or overhead cost, is actually, for a contractor, a variable cost. Liability insurance is figured as a percentage of gross revenues <u>and</u> as a percentage of payroll <u>and</u> as a percentage of payments to subcontractors .[25] Therefore some contractors include a separate line item for liability insurance. The gross revenues portion includes overhead and profit charges, so that portion of the premium must be calculated <u>after</u> calculating overhead and profit.

## Performance Bond.

**138**

The same goes for a performance bond[26] fee, which is calculated on the <u>entire</u> contract amount. Therefore, a bond fee is either added <u>after</u> overhead

---

[25] The combined total is the insurance premium charge.

[26] A performance bond (also known as a completion bond and usually shortened to just "bond") is really just an insurance policy guarantying that a project will be completed. An owner has no assurance when he receives a bid, or enters a contract, that the bidder can actually perform the work for the amount of money bid or set in the contract. To guarantee that the contractor can actually complete the project, an owner can ask for a performance bond from an independent insurer. By providing a bond, the insurer (known as the surety) commits to step in and complete the project if the contractor defaults or fails in some way; usually by hiring another contractor to finish the work, although they may fund completion by the original contractor. Then the surety seeks to recover from the contractor's assets. Only financially sound contractors are able to obtain bonds.

A companion bond usually obtained at the same time is a payment bond. This bond assures that all bills are paid. A payment bond is protection against liens (see page 173).

Performance bonding, although common in commercial work, is rare in residential work and almost non-existent in remodeling projects. Bond fees are in the .25% to 3% range of the total contract amount.

and profit, or excluded from the contract with the proviso that, if the owner desires a performance bond, he will pay the premium outside of the contract.

## Variable Overhead

Other variations are charges for general supervision, shop drawings, timekeeping and other items that are directly job related, but are performed by home office employees on salary. Sometimes these costs are allocated to the job in overhead; sometimes they are set forth as separate line items. These types of variations may or may not affect the percentage rate a general contractor charges. The more of these types of items entered as individual line items, the lower the overhead amount should be.

**139**

## Margins

Most homebuilders and remodelers will range between 10% – 20% for overhead; and 5% - 15% for profit on prime contract competitive bids. They may drop lower, but seldom below 15% combined, depending upon whether they need work, or are fully booked. (You will always get better pricing when builders need work.) Anything less than 15% concerns me as being too low to support overhead and earn the builder a fair profit. Larger jobs may go at lower margins, while smaller jobs need higher margins to justify the risk and commitment.

## Change Orders.

While you may not know the overhead and profit margins your contractor has written into his original bid, you must set rates for change orders ("CO"s). Change order markup rates should be fixed in the prime contract. Since change orders are negotiated, and the builder is already on the job and familiar with jobsite conditions, the risk is generally considered lower than when bidding the original contract. Often the work is authorized on a time and materials basis. The markup for a fixed price change order should be no more than 15% - 17.5% combined; for time and materials[27] COs lower rates can be negotiated, even 10% or less. There may be a minimum fee for a change order. Contractors who employ salespersons (often referred to as design consultants) must build in a commission. The going rate is 8% - 10%.

## Lump Sum Margins

In lump sum bids and contracts[28], other than for change orders, you don't care or need to know what the margins are. You will make your decision by comparing the total amount bid by each bidder to the total amount bid by the other bidders.

## Negotiated Contracts Margins

In negotiated work how margins are fixed, and what they are, is of direct concern to you. Basically in negotiated work the contractor is theoretically decreasing his risk. Be aware of some tricks. While a contractor may negotiate with a markup of 10 and 5, for instance, he may be self-performing a lot of labor and charging inflated rates.

## Stated Labor Rates in Negotiated Contracts and Change Orders

Look carefully at not only the cost of a self-performed activities, but at the total labor hours estimated and the labor rates – do they pass the reasonableness test. Don't forget to allow for contingencies and risk. If your

---

[27] Also referred to as cost-plus or simply "T&M".

[28] See page 146 for a discussion of contract types.

contractor wants to charge you, say, $75.00 per hour for a carpenter, don't necessarily accept that at face value. Ask what the base wage rate is, then do the arithmetic to calculate the employer's payroll burden:

7.65% for social security and medicare

5.25% for unemployment insurance (on the first $7,000 earned annually)

15% - 25% or more for workers compensation insurance, depending on the trade (you can look up rates for your state online)

1% more or less for health care

But how do you know how much a carpenter earns in your area. Again, go online and search for "prevailing wage rates" for your area. These are tables published by the federal government which set the minimum wages that must be paid on federal jobs. These rates are based upon union labor rates, so they are typically somewhat higher than non-union rates.

So, if the base prevailing wage for a journeyman carpenter is $23.50 per hour, his total cost to his employer would be another $14.45 per hour for a total cost of $37.95. If your contractor is totaling up all his costs and then marking them up, then that's it. Clearly, $75.00 per hour would be excessive. Remember, some master tradesmen will earn more; apprentices will earn less. You will need to dig into it. This is an area which is very difficult for the amateur to negotiate; you would do well to seek the help of an owner rep.

You will need to go through the same kind of exercise with materials.

One final thing to be aware of is the rule of markups: to achieve a 20% margin, the base costs must be marked up 25%. Example: $80 x 25% = $100.

The margin is calculated as $100 - $80 = $20, which is 20% of $100.

# THE CONSTRUCTION CONTRACT

# CONTRACTS

The construction contract is an important document and care should be taken regarding its preparation and execution. It often involves a large sum of money, as well as an unknown – the future performance of the contractor. If that future performance is not carefully defined, you may find yourself exposed to losses or damages that you cannot afford.

---

### DO I NEED A LAWYER?

How much do you know about construction contracting?

Have you ever negotiated a contract before?

How much do you trust your builder?

How much money is at stake?

Do you feel lucky today?

---

There are many, many different construction contracts. Some are many pages long; others just a page or two. Home improvement in many states, such as California, is heavily regulated with much mandatory language that must be included in home improvement contracts. If your state has a license board you should be able to find requirements for home improvement contracts on their website. Home improvement generally refers to work on an already existing home or condominium apartment lived in by the owner. New home construction, or homes or apartments owned for commercial purposes – *i.e.*, for rent – are generally not subject to regulated contracts.

In general a construction contract will describe the work to be performed, provide a date by which the work shall be completed and describe the scope of the work to be performed. There will usually be a section or addendum entitled "General Conditions" which is basically just what it sounds like. Attached as exhibits will be the working drawings, the written specifications, a schedule of values and a performance schedule – although sometimes the contract calls for the last two to be submitted later for approval by the owner. The contract will state whether the owner is representing himself, or whether he has appointed a representative to deal with the contractor. The contract should have a change order clause, stating that no changes shall be made absent an amendment (the change order) in writing signed by both parties. It will set forth the conditions upon which payment is earned, whether retainage is to be withheld, and the terms of payment, including lien waiver requirements. There will be a section addressing dispute resolution.[29] And, of course, it sets forth the price.

**146**

## CONTRACT TYPES

There are a number of basic contract types:

### Lump Sum

The contractor agrees to build a project with a specific scope of work for a fixed price. A lump-sum contract is suitable if the scope and schedule of the project are sufficiently defined to allow the contractor to fully estimate project costs. This is the most common and traditional contract type.

---

[29] See page 217 for a discussion of dispute resolution.

## Cost Plus

Cost plus is a contract agreement wherein the owner agrees to pay the cost of the work, including all subcontractors, labor, materials, and equipment, plus an amount for the general contractor's overhead and profit, and the contractor organizes and manages the project. The amount paid to the contractor may be a percentage of the costs, or it may be a fixed fee.

Cost plus contracts are favored where the scope of work is indeterminate or highly uncertain, and the kinds of labor, material, and equipment needed are also uncertain – such as an extensive remodel where the client is uncertain how far they wish to go, or which lacks a fully developed set of plans. Basically, a pay as you go arrangement.

147

In cost plus all financial risk is retained by the owner in exchange for a lower fee by the builder. The builder's fee is usually in the single digits, sometimes less than five percent, depending on what services are to be included in the fee. Sometimes supervision is included, in which case the fee is higher, both to compensate for the direct cost of the supervising employee, but also for the risk of extra expense due to non-compensated time over-runs.

In cost plus the contractor conducts the project just as if he were a fixed fee contractor; that is, he purchases all materials and contracts for all services and subcontractors. He bills the owner and then pays the bills. The owner has only one contract relationship – with the prime contractor.

Although this sounds like a way to hold costs down, in percentage fee (cost plus) contracts the builder has no incentive to keep costs down. If the fee is percentage based, the greater the costs, the more he earns; the lower the costs, the less he earns. In the fixed fee format, however, the contractor earns the same amount regardless of the costs. He has no incentive to either keep costs down or to drive costs up. He does have an incentive to quickly finish the project because the quicker he completes the job, the greater his incremental earnings.

The biggest problem with percentage fee or cost plus is tension between the owner and builder. Owners may begin to minutely review and challenge every bill presented by the builder. This can lead to hours of argument and dispute, ultimately poisoning the relationship between the builder and the owner and even leading to litigation. An owner putting a clock on workers may not consider that the worker first had to stop at Home Depot, where he spent an hour picking up materials, or may be delayed by another trade, but still must be paid for being on the job. Only if the owner and builder have complete trust and confidence in each other should a cost plus contract be considered.

**148**

## Fee Basis Management

Fee basis management is a variation of cost plus where the owner contracts directly with the vendors and pays the bills directly, but the work is managed by the contractor for a fee. The fee may either be fixed for the project, or be time based – such as daily, weekly or monthly. It may also be task based, such as through foundation, or for finishes. Many large contractors have different superintendents for different phases of a project. An owner considering this method should be cautioned that the owner must obtain and maintain liability and builder's risk insurance, write payroll for any directly employed laborers, and enter and manage multiple contracts.

## Guaranteed Maximum Price

A variation is cost plus with a guaranteed maximum. This gives incentive to the contractor to hold costs below the maximum because he is responsible for any cost overruns. This is usually more effective when coupled with a savings sharing clause wherein the savings spread between actual costs and the guaranteed maximum is split between the contractor and the owner. This type of contract can be beneficial in complex remodels because the builder can price in his risk for unknowns, but if those costs are not actually incurred, the savings accrue to, or are shared with, the owner.

## Unit Price

This kind of contract is based on estimated quantities of items included in the project and their unit prices; in other words, so much for each brick, for instance, put in place by the contractor. The final price of the project is dependent on the quantities actually put in place. In general, this contract is only suitable for projects in which the scope is reasonably well established, and the different types of items (but not their numbers) can be accurately identified in the contract documents. Unit price contracts are often found in earthwork and utilities construction contracts, but are rarely, if ever used, in residential construction.

149

## Cost-Reimbursable Alternative

This is simply a hybrid of lump sum and cost plus. The contractor is paid for the work with a mix of reimbursable items (cost plus) and fixed fees. Cost-reimbursable alternative contracts are effective when the general scope of work and schedule are defined, but there is uncertainty in quantities or execution of certain, but not all, portions of the work. An example would be a rural house with a very long driveway. The house itself could be lump sum, while the grading and paving the driveway could be based upon actual quantities of or time spent grading and paving.

# THE CONTRACT DOCUMENTS

> "A verbal contract is not worth the paper it's written on."
>
> - Sam Goldwyn

**150**

There are a number of exhibits which are typically attached to a construction contract. Taken together they, if properly prepared, clearly set for the obligations, rights and expectations of the parties: what is to be done, how it is to be done, who is to do what, when it is to be started and finished. They also address insurance requirements, dispute resolution and other matters of importance.

The include Special Conditions, General Conditions, Scope of Work, List of Drawings, List of Vendors, Progress Schedule, Schedule of Values, Payment Request form and Lien Waiver form.

Incorporated by reference will be the Working Drawings and the Specifications. The Working Drawings should be initialed by each party to the contract, as there are usually multiple iterations of plans for any project and, as the plans define the work, it is important to know which set of plans is the basis for the contract.

Some contractors like to initial every contract page and exhibit. This is not a bad idea.

You should have two sets of the contract documents and plans with original (or "wet") signatures – one for you and one for your contractor. Lenders, if involved, will usually accept copies.

## CRITICAL COMPONENTS OF A CONSTUCTION CONTRACT

- Names of the parties
- Addresses and contact information for the parties
- Address of the project site
- Description of the work
- Contract price
- Payment terms and liens
- Time for starting and completing the work
- Drawings and specifications
- List of contract documents
- Contractor's rights and responsibilities
- Owner's rights and responsibilities
- Insurance
- Damage or destruction of the improvements
- Site conditions
- Asbestos/hazardous materials
- Hidden conditions
- Material removed and debris
- Extra work and variable cost items
- Allowances
- Compliance with the plans and codes
- Inspection and testing
- Permits and fees

151

**152**

## CRITICAL COMPONENTS OF A CONSTUCTION CONTRACT (cont.)

- Materials and finishes selections
- List of owner supplied fixtures and equipment
- Permits and fees
- Taxes
- Corrective work and punchlist
- Warranty
- Legal notices
- Marketing permissions
- Severance; governing law
- Dispute resolution
- Attorneys' fees
- Quality of materials
- Substitutions
- Statutory disclosures
- Lien law disclosure

### EXHIBITS

- Plans
- Specifications
- Progress schedule
- Schedule of values
- Materials and finishes selections
- List of owner supplied fixtures and equipment

# THE ESSENTIAL ELEMENTS OF A CONSTRUCTION CONTRACT

## Who

A contract must name the parties who are making the agreement. Addresses to which notices are to be sent should be set forth.

## What

The contract must describe what the agreement is. In construction that would be what building work the one party, identified as the "Contractor", agrees to be perform or deliver for the benefit of the other party, the "Owner", and how much the Owner agrees to pay the Contractor in exchange.

153

There you have it – a meeting of the minds and consideration – the basic elements that make a contract. You could proceed just like that, but that would be foolish. A good contract will spell out conditions, provide ways to solve future events that might affect the basic agreement, and how to resolve disputes.

## When

Set forth when the work is to start, what event triggers the start of work, what conditions must be met before the work can be started, and a date by which the work must be completed. If the work is not completed on time, provide for liquidated damages.[30]

---

[30] If your project is not completed when you anticipate, you will incur costs, most of which are hard to pinpoint or calculate exactly – such as extra interest, rent, meals out, cancelled vacation. Rather than try to identify all these costs and value them, an amount of money is pre-determined as fair compensation – thus "liquidating" the losses. Many construction

## Description of the Work

Provide a detailed description of the work to be performed. This is usually done by reference to a clearly identified set of plans (by architect's name, date, revision number) and specifications. The plans are identified as an exhibit to the contract (such as "Exhibit 1") and the phrase "included herein by this reference" makes clear that they are intended to be an integral part of the contract agreement between the parties. Often a detailed Scope of Work will also be prepared and attached.

## Contract Price and Terms of Payment

The contract amount is usually set forth as a separate clause in the contract. The terms of payment should also be defined – when payment is earned and how much. This may be a simple statement such as "the fee shall be paid monthly in an amount equal to the percentage of the work completed". As you can imagine, this is vague and subject to interpretation; and anything subject to interpretation is subject to dispute.

Or it can be set as a specified amount of money upon the completion of certain defined milestones – such as X amount upon completion of the foundation.

For larger, extended projects the best method is to attach a schedule of values, usually based upon MasterFormat, which assigns a value for each of the significant line items in the budget – such as carpentry, drywall, painting, etc. – and provide that payment shall be made monthly as a percentage of completion of each of those items. The larger a line item is, the more important to break it down into manageable components. This can be tricky, however, for the

---

advisors believe it fair when imposing liquidated damages, or "LD's", to offer an early completion incentive. Thus, LD's might be $125 per day and an early completion bonus might be $100 per day.

inexperienced and is a perfect example of an instance where an experienced construction advisor is well worth the fee.

Never agree to pay fixed amounts on pre-set dates without basis in the work actually completed.

Care must be taken that the payment schedule is not "front loaded" by the contractor. A contractor will always want to get as much money upfront as he can, and you will want to hold as much money as you can. Do not try to squeeze your contractor, but do not let him get ahead of you. A small mobilization fee is fair – he has home office expenses getting ready to start work, he needs to set up the field office and portable toilet; the excavator may have significant trucking time hauling in his equipment. I would recommend engaging an experienced consultant to help you craft a fair and balanced schedule of values.

Retention (also called retainage) is an amount of money withheld by the owner from a payment otherwise earned to protect against defects in the work which may not become apparent until later. Out of plumb framing or warped studs may not be discovered until the tile guy begins work. This amount is usually 5% - 10% of the payment amount. The difficulty here is that your contractor may be working on a 10% - 15% margin, which means 10% retainage may leave him with less money than he needs to pay for his overhead. Retainage should be held for a specific purpose and for a specific time. For instance, 10% of the foundation could be held until the first floor framing is complete. By then you will know if the foundation is square and level and there is not a legitimate reason for continuing to hold your contractor's money. Retainage should be legitimate and fair and promptly released when no reason remains for holding it.

A retention clause will be resisted by your contractor. An alternative is no retainage, but the right to withhold from future payments, for whatever reason earned, if an issue arises. Just be sure that you have a final line item which is due only "upon completion". Clearly define what completion is.

> Remember – once you pay, it's gone.  Do not allow yourself to be overbilled.

In many states, such as California, overbilling for home improvements is actually illegal.  Regardless, once you overpay you have a problem.

## Contingency Fund

In a fixed price contract, your builder will have built into his price an amount of money for contingencies.  A contingency fund pays for those things he missed, or that take more time and work or cost more than he anticipated.  A contractor's contingency line item pays for his errors or omissions.

In a negotiated contract the contingency fund will be a separate line item.  However, since you are reimbursing your contractor all the costs he incurs, he has no need of a contingency.  But you do.  What if the excavator runs into solid granite and it costs twice as much to excavate the footings.  You have to pay, since, with a negotiated contract, you accepted the risk.  You need to have some amount of money in reserve.

Sometimes a contract is written for a fixed amount plus an amount for contingencies.  You will need to define very carefully under what circumstances the contractor gets to draw upon the contingency.  If he runs over on a line item, can he draw; or is it only for costs outside of the identified line items?  If he can draw if he goes over on a category, must return any cost savings on line items that came in less than budgeted?

These are some of the permutations a contingency fund can take.  The important thing to take away is to be prepared, to a greater or lesser degree, for cost overruns.  It is the rare project that ends up costing less than planned.

## Contractor's Rights and Responsibilities; Owner's Rights and Responsibilities

What can you do if the contractor fails to show up or abandons the work? What he can do if you don't pay him. Where the workers park; radio noise; cursing; work hours – these are some of the general topics that need to be addressed. Address the conditions of and approvals or limits on the contractor's right to subcontract work; or to substitute subcontractors once approved. You should always retain the right to approve subcontractors.

## Change Orders

**157**

Set forth a procedure for dealing with changes to the work. See page 182 for a full discussion about Change Orders.

## Insurance and Damage or Destruction of the Work

What happens if the project burns down half-way through or a worker falls off the roof? It's critical that you have the right insurance to protect yourself – both that which you obtain for yourself, and that which your contractor must maintain to protect both himself and you. See the discussion beginning on page 188.

Give yourself the right to obtain insurance on behalf of your contractor, or pay his premiums, if he fails to maintain coverage and to deduct the cost from payments otherwise earned by him.

## Hidden Conditions; Hazardous Materials

What to do if solid granite is found three feet down into the basement excavation. What if termites have eaten away a beam the contractor exposes that the architect assumed would support the new work; what if it isn't even there? What if toxic waste is discovered on the site?

## Materials

Require that all materials be new unless specified otherwise.

**158**

## Employees

Require that your contractor comply with all employment laws and regulations, including worker's compensation, payroll reporting, non-discrimination and equal opportunity. Require that all workers be on payroll. Many small contractors will attempt to circumvent payroll taxes and reporting requirements by treating workers as "1099" independent contractors.[31] A worker rarely, if ever, qualifies as an independent contractor. To be an independent contractor, at a minimum, they should be licensed (contractor's license and business license), have obtained an EIN[32] from the Internal Revenue Service, provide their own tools, set their own means and methods of executing the work, set their own schedule, receive income from other sources. You may also require your contractor to provide proof that all payroll taxes have been paid. In the event union workers are used on your project, you will want to verify that all trust fund obligations are met.

---

[31] 1099 refers to IRS form 1099 used to report monies paid to independent contractors.

[32] Employer Identification Number.

You should also address standards of behavior on the jobsite and reserve the right to have removed any worker you find offensive (you must describe the causes). I always prohibit smoking in a building after framing. For remodel work, smoking is prohibited, period. Personally, I would prohibit smoking at all times, but this can create friction at the earthwork, foundation, framing and roofing stages.

## Safety

Jobsite safety is very important. Detached residential construction has some of the higher workers' compensation rates. That, in itself, tells you something about how important safety is. While large contractors and large construction sites have formal safety programs and even safety officers, small, isolated projects seldom do. Failure to address safety issues in an aggressive manner is one of the most significant failures of small residential contractors.

Require that your contractor have a safety plan and require that a copy be kept on the jobsite. Require a first aid kit and require that it be maintained. Know where the nearest hospital is. Set a few basic rules and see that they are enforced. These are: fall protection, leading edge protocol, shoes, saw guards, electrical hazards, ladders. Hard hats I'm not so concerned with, but sometimes they are appropriate. I don't really care if the tile guy has a hardhat, or the roofer. But it is probably a good idea for the framers and certainly for anyone working below a hazard. Do not store flammable materials or rags inside buildings (built or in progress).

Material safety data sheets (MSDS) should be required of the painters, anyone using glue or chemicals, from the supplier of treated lumber, from the landscaper. Keep them in a binder on the jobsite.

Keep your jobsite clean. That means *at all times* during the course of the work, not just at the end of the week, or even just at the end of the day. No debris underfoot, no nails sticking up, no piles of debris or lunch trash laying around. Require that the project be kept broom clean on a daily basis and that debris be regularly and promptly disposed of. Require debris receptacles.

Expect that your project will be visited by a state or federal safety inspector. Paying attention to these few simple areas will go a long way to getting you through any safety inspection. Remember, anything which becomes a problem for your contractor, ultimately becomes a problem for you.

## Compliance with Codes

**160**

Require that the work be built in compliance with all codes regardless of the representations in the plans and specifications. (You should tie this into the plans contract – if it is the architect's error, should the contractor be responsible for finding it and cross checking to codes, or is that the architect's responsibility? Who pays? The contractor, the architect...or you?)

## Inspection and Testing

Who is responsible for obtaining the building permit? Paying for it? Who calls for inspections; who pays for special inspections and tests? Reserve your right to test any work and require that the contractor pay for any failed tests.

## Allowances and Selections

These are amounts of money included in the contract price that are reserved to purchase certain items to be incorporated into the work which are subject to aesthetic choices and the cost of which can vary significantly, based upon your choices – typically light fixtures, flooring, tile, and the like. If an allowance item costs less than the allowance amount, you get a credit against the contract price; it if comes in over, you write a check. Actual installation is usually included in the contract fixed price. Similar are selections such as paint colors. Deadlines should be set for informing the contractor of your choices.

## Taxes

What taxes are you responsible for and which are the responsibility of the contractor.

## Corrective Work, Punchlist and Warranty

This ties into the payment schedule (aka the schedule of values). Provide that no payment is due for defective work, that the contractor must remove and replace all defective work (whenever, or even if, it is pointed out to him) at no cost to you, that money can be withheld until completion of punchlist[33] items. Be sure specific language makes the contractor responsible for the work of all his subcontractors and the quality and compliance of all materials.

Require a warranty and set the terms and scope thereof. Provide that the contractor assemble and deliver to you – in clean, pristine condition – all product and equipment literature, manuals and warranties. Have language that assigns all the contractor's rights to warranty benefits to you. Define the term and the start date of the warranty. One, preferably two years is typical for workmanship. Materials vary, and often come with a manufacturer's warranty. Many states have a ten year statutory warranty on structural elements.

---

[33] A punchlist is a list of items that fail to pass inspection or which are not completed. A punchlist is typically agreed to between the owner and the contractor during a walk-through of the project. Often the walk will be conducted by the architect or construction manager – which is a good idea. It is nice to have an intermediary when differences of opinion are possible.

## Dispute Resolution

Going in none of us (usually) expect to have trouble, but we are wise to anticipate how to resolve trouble when it happens. Also state which laws govern the contract, how to handle attorneys' fees, and venue. See the chapter in the Construction Section on Dispute Resolution.

## Miscellaneous

Drafting of the contract, assignment, succession, statutory disclosures, headings and other boilerplate.

---

### ALERT

The preceding is only a summary of the many issues which need to be addressed in a competent construction contract. A good contract is your number one tool to a successful, smooth-running and trouble free project. It is also your first line of defense in the event of problems or disputes. Consult a good construction manager or construction attorney to be sure you have a comprehensive and competent contract. It will keep you out of trouble — guaranteed!

---

# CONTRACT BILLINGS

At the core of the contract, about which everything else revolves, is the exchange of money for services. A certain amount of money for certain (hopefully) clearly defined services.

It is important to understand a little bit about how your contractor will bill you for the work he performs.

The bid and the contract itself are usually single, lump sum numbers – say $100,000. Even if a contractor had the necessary working capital to fund your entire construction project until completion, he does not want to be your banker. So he will ask for progress payments along the way. This is standard procedure. Larger contracts are typically billed monthly; smaller projects may be billed in their entirety at completion. Likewise, larger, more established contractors usually have larger amounts of working capital compared to smaller contractors. Thus, smaller contractors may suggest a bi-monthly, or even weekly, payment schedule – especially if a job is larger or longer than their normal project. This does not necessarily mean they are less competent, it simply means they have a shorter cycle on their working capital.

However, if a contractor asks for a weekly billing *and* he is the lowest bidder – especially if he is significantly lower – it could mean that he has underbid your job; or consistently underbids his jobs and is chronically short of cash. Special care must be taken with a contractor who is under-capitalized. Lack of adequate capitalization will cause cash flow problems, which can lead to problems for you.

When a contractor has cash flow problems, he will have problems paying his bills in a timely manner and will often rob Peter to pay Paul. He may use money from your job to pay bills on another job; or to make his truck payment. The money you pay to your contractor for work done by his

163

workmen or subcontractors is NOT his money; he is actually holding that money in trust for the persons to whom the money is actually payable. Upon accepting such money he becomes a "trustee", a term which, in most states, has legal meaning. In some states, such as Colorado, it is a statutory crime punishable by jail time to divert contract payments collected on behalf of workers, suppliers or subcontractors to other uses. In other states, such as California, redress must be sought under the trusteeship laws.

Although commingling of funds is usually permitted, careful accounting procedures must be used to assure that your money goes only where it is supposed to go. It is important that you have at least a general idea of your contractor's financial capacity and accounting sophistication. Feel free to ask him how he handles this issue; and about his accounting staff, just as you should inquire about the supervisor assigned to your project.

It is possible for a contractor to manage his cash flow and execute a project with very little working capital. But, just as he does not want to be your banker, you don't want to be his banker. Pay only for that work which is in place. This leads us to the Schedule of Values.

## Schedule of Values

The Schedule of Values ("SOV") breaks the work of a project down into its components, to a greater or lesser degree, and assigns each of the components (usually referred to as a "line item") a dollar value, the total of which adds up to the contract amount. The Schedule of Values is the basis for contract billings.

The line item values in a Schedule of Values is often different from the line item values in an estimate or bid. In an estimate the various line items (labor, materials, subcontractors) are valued at their actual cost to the contractor; then the contractor totals all the costs to arrive at a total job cost.

The total job cost is different than the bid amount, because to the total job cost the contractor adds his costs of supervision, insurance, general company overhead allocation and profit. In the Schedule of Values the contractor distributes these items equitably among all of the individual line items to arrive at billing values.

Schedules of Values are often submitted for approval after the contract is signed, but, in my opinion, a well written bid request will require that the Schedule of Values be submitted after award but prior to, and as a condition precedent, to signing the contract. That way any disagreement over the values is resolved before the parties become bound to each other.

Some contractors will attempt to "front load" the Schedule of Values. They do this by assigning an inflated value to early tasks in the timeline of the job, thus leaving the later tasks undervalued. If this is allowed, the homeowner might find that in the later stages of the contract the cost to complete the remaining work exceeds the amount of unpaid money left in the contract sum. This is a situation you do not want to find yourself in – especially with an under-capitalized contractor.

**165**

## Materials Delivered

Although legitimate, making payment for materials before they are incorporated in the project is risky for the homeowner.[34]  If you pay for materials in advance of their being incorporated into the project, you are at risk of monetary loss should those materials disappear or be damaged before they are installed.

If asked to pay for materials in advance insist on protections for yourself.  First, the materials should be delivered and stored only on the jobsite, not at the contractor's yard.  Inventory the materials (either yourself or your owner's representative; don't take the contractor's word, no matter how much you trust him) so that there will be no question as to what, and how much, was delivered to the jobsite.  Take photographs.  The jobsite should be secured with a fence and other security as might be appropriate, such as lights or alarms.  In some instances it may be appropriate to store materials off-site, such as appliances or equipment, hardware or fixtures; but, if you do, they must be stored in a secure location.  And they must also be inventoried.

All materials delivered on or off site should be insured against loss (including fire, storm, theft or vandalism) by the contractor's liability policy.  A prudent owner will also maintain a policy of construction risk during the course of the project.

Payment for materials delivered should only be for the invoice amount and cost of third party delivery.  No, or negligible supervision, is incurred nor any overhead or profit earned until the materials are incorporated into the work.

---

[34] In California, among other states, it is illegal for a home improvement contractor to ask for or receive payment for materials before they are delivered to the jobsite.  Note that this restriction does not apply to new home construction or commercial projects.

An alternate method of security is to deposit the cost of materials with a third party to be held in trust and disbursed to the contractor at such time as the materials are incorporated. Such a willing and acceptable party may be hard to find, however, and the procedure may not be acceptable to the contractor who is faced, on his side, with making payment to his supplier.

## Special Order Items

A similar situation exists when a contractor seeks payment for special order items. Examples would be cabinets or granite countertops. In my opinion it is legitimate for the contractor to seek payment for these items, because once he orders them, he is committed to the supplier to take delivery and pay for them even if you, the owner, decide later not to pay him for them (regardless of your reason[35]). This is because these items are made or fabricated to order and will have no, or diminished value, to any other person.

In California and other states, regardless of the expense to the contractor, it is nevertheless illegal for him to collect[36] payment for special order items prior to their delivery to the jobsite. This puts the contractor at risk (unfairly in the minds of most contractors) for sometimes substantial amounts of money. One way they will attempt to compensate for this is by front loading their Schedules of Value – such as for demolition or grading. In new home contracts, the restriction does not exist. Another solution is to break these items out of the contract and have the homeowner purchase them directly and deliver them to the contractor for installation.

---

[35] Changing your mind is not a legitimate reason.

[36] Or, in California, even to ask.

## Approving the Schedule of Values

Schedules of Values are usually established in the following format:

| Description | Value | # of Units | Unit of Measure | Units (or %) Complete | Amount Earned | Less Previous Payments | Current Balance Due | Amount to Finish |
|---|---|---|---|---|---|---|---|---|
| Task | $5,000 | 2500 | SF | 50% | $2,500 | $500 | $2,000 | $2,500 |

Sometimes the units statements are omitted in favor of simple percentage of completion. I believe it is always wise to use units of measure whenever possible, because it provides an absolute scale to determine the percentage complete. Otherwise percentage complete is subjective and open to disagreement.

The Current Balance Due is calculated as the Value x Percent Complete = Amount Earned. Current Due is simply Amount Earned minus Previous Payments. Balance to Finish is Value minus Amount Earned. Balance to Finish is a nice check on the Percent Complete. If it doesn't seem like the Balance to Complete is sufficient to complete the work, then the Percentage Complete must be over-stated.[37]

As is probably clear by now, the Schedule of Values is a key contract management tool; and it is also subject to manipulation by clever or experienced contractors. While this won't necessarily get you into trouble, it very easily could. I strongly advise, except for small single or double payment improvement projects, that most homeowners retain the services of a qualified

---

[37] This is true even if the previous payments are made on the basis of suppliers actual invoices. This would indicate that the value is understated. This may be due to bid error – in which case you need to stay especially alert to the overall money left in the contract; you may need to withhold money elsewhere to protect yourself. Your contract should give you the right to protect yourself in this manner.

independent construction manager or owner's representative to review and approve any proposed contract Schedule of Values prior to acceptance; and to review and recommend (either approval or modification) payment requests.

Change Orders should be added as separate line items sequentially at the end of the Schedule of Values. Even if the change may be to add additional quantities to an existing line item, it is generally confusing to change the amount of a line item in the middle of the project. The effect on the SOV of adjusting line items is to adjust the total contract amount without reference to the actual Change Orders. This is confusing. I strongly recommend keeping Change Orders separate, even if that means billing parallel percentages with the original line item. It absolutely avoids confusion.

**169**

## PAYMENT REQUESTS

The Schedule of Values is the backup document to the Payment Request, which is the actual bill or invoice. A well formatted Payment Request will be set up as follows:

Request #
Date

Original Contract Amount
+ Total Amount of Previous Change Orders
+ Total Change Orders this Request
= Total Revised Contract Amount

Percent Complete
= Total Earned Job to Date
- Retainage (if any)
- Previous Billed
= Current Due

Balance to Complete

The Payment Request (also commonly referred to as a Draw or Draw Request) will also state the contractor's name and address, the owner's name and address, and often the architect, construction manager or other pertinent information. The Schedule of Values is the basis for the Payment Request and should be attached thereto.[38] Typically the Payment Request has a statement to the effect that the percentage being billed is an accurate representation of the actual work in place and that work being billed has been completed in compliance with the plans, specifications and applicable building codes and regulations, with space for the contractor's signature certifying that statement.

If there is a third party inspector reviewing, approving or certifying the billing, he or she will also sign the request. There should also be a statement that all obligations represented by previous Payment Requests have been paid in full.

**170**

## PAYING THE BILLS

It is incumbent upon you, as the homeowner, to protect your property against liens and to assure that the money you disburse goes where it is supposed to. Although you can get conditional lien waivers, you have no real way of knowing until the next billing cycle if the money you are disbursing gets to the right place.

There are a number of ways to protect yourself.

First, be sure your contract requires your contractor to provide you a list of vendors and subcontractors. Know who is on your job. Require your contractor to provide subcontractor waivers to you in his progress billing

---

[38] Commonly used are AIA forms G702 and G703.

packages. Keep track of the preliminary notices[39] and match them to the lien waivers he provides you.

Check with the vendors and subs to make sure they are being paid in a timely manner.

Have your contractor provide proof that he has paid his payroll taxes.

Pay with joint checks.

Use a funds control service.

# 171

## Joint Checks

Joint checks are a simple control you can use yourself to assure that all your contractor's suppliers and subcontractors are paid. Always reserve the right to do this in your prime contract; it doesn't mean you have to, but you retain the right if, at some point, you feel you need to.

A joint check is made payable to both the contractor and his subcontractor or supplier; it cannot be cashed without both their signatures. Normally the contractor simply endorses it over to the vendor. Be sure to obtain lien waivers just like for any other payment you make.

You will need to contact the vendor to determine the amount he claims to be owed, then confirm that amount with your contractor. Hopefully they agree; if not, then you must referee a resolution. (In the meantime you should pay the undisputed amount.) Two problems occur: first, the contractor takes offense that you are stepping into his management of his business relationship; second, usually in the instance of a fixed price contract, he doesn't want you to

---

[39] See page 176.

know the particulars of what he is paying his vendor – thinking that you can then calculate how much he is making.  In reality it doesn't matter since you presumably selected his bid from more than one competitive bid; you can't go back and renegotiate.

In the event of a negotiated contract, you presumably had access to that information during the negotiation.  What you could discover is that your contractor then *re-negotiated* the price down with his vendor and did not pass the savings along to you.  Your contract should address this issue.

## 172 Funds Control

Using a funds control service is another way to ensure payment.  Many lumber yards will provide funds control, and there are also independent services.  Caution – be sure the funds control service is bonded.  Many lenders will insist that funds control be used.

The funds control will receive the progress payment request and inspect the work for completeness.  When they authorize the disbursement it will be made by you, or your lender, to them rather than to the contractor.  The contractor will prepare checks to the vendors on a special funds control account and deliver those checks to the funds control who will log the checks, fund the account and mail the checks. The contractor receives the remainder.  You will be charged a fee for the inspection and control service, but you are virtually assured that your money is being used for the purpose you intend.

### Retainage

Many contracts provide that a portion of the earned value of the work be withheld to fund omissions not noticed prior to completion, or corrections that become apparent later. This amount is known as retainage or retention. The amount varies from 5% - 10%. Some contracts hold 10% through 50% of the project and nothing thereafter. Other contracts may reserve the right to hold retainage, but conditionally waive actually holding any. Retainage is usually held for a short period after substantial completion of the project – usually 45 to 90 days. The hold period is often tied to the filing deadline for liens. If retainage is held from the general contractor, he will hold a like amount from his subcontractors.

If a contractor desires to withhold retainage from his subs, but you are not withholding retainage from him, then he is holding any monies received in trust. A better arrangement would be for the prime contract to require him to notify you if he desires retainage withheld, and you hold the money.

173

In long contracts it is reasonable to release retainage along the way. For instance, the concrete foundation contractor should not have retainage held until the project is complete. That could be months. The risk of exposure due to his work usually ends once framing is underway. So once your, and your contractor's potential liability is cleared it is only fair that the retainage be released.

Well written contracts will provide additional causes to withhold money. Most common of these is to pay for insurance premiums or payroll tax withholdings if your contractor fails to do so.

## CONSTRUCTION LIENS

A construction lien is an encumbrance (claim) against your property, in the same manner as a mortgage. However, it takes precedence in payment to a mortgage or any other voluntary encumbrance (but is subordinate to tax liens) and you will, therefore, not be able to obtain a home loan if there is a construction lien filed on your property. Also, if your construction is being funded by a bank or other lender, that lender will insist upon resolution of the lien prior to advancing any further project funds; in fact, they may even step in and pay the lien themselves if you fail to resolve it. Good communication is imperative.

## Who Can File a Lien

**174**

There are two types of construction liens: mechanic's and materialman's. From your perspective as a homeowner, they have exactly the same effect – they encumber your property. A mechanic's lien may be filed by any person or business that has performed labor or services towards the improvement of your real property. This includes improvements to the land itself, such as grading or underground utilities, as well as actual buildings. A materialman's lien is available to any business or person who has delivered materials to your jobsite which are intended to be incorporated into the real improvements. The materialman must have actually delivered the materials to the site, either himself or by using the services of a third party delivery service. Materials purchased by your contractor or his subcontractors and picked up by them offsite and then taken onsite are included in their "services" and thus can be included in their mechanic's lien, but not be subject to a separate materialman's lien.

Anyone who provides services or materials to your project may generally be entitled to file a lien, even payroll workers. In some states non-licensed persons acting as contractors are barred from having lien rights. They generally retain the right to pursue any claims by lawsuit or arbitration.

It is important to note that the lien is only a statement of a claim alerting anyone who may, or may potentially have, a financial interest in your property

the construction contract

to the claim being made by the lienor. It effectively makes your real property collateral for the eventual claim. The lienor must generally go to court to "prove up" the lien within a set period of time or it will be automatically dismissed. Proving up means providing the court with sufficient proof of cause that a potentially legitimate claim exits, at which time the lien becomes perfected. The lienor then must initiate litigation to win his claim, at which time, if he prevails, the mechanic's (or materialman's) lien converts to a judgment lien.

Usually there is a statutory limit to the time a claimant has to file a lien or his lien rights automatically expire. This does not mean his legal rights expire, however, and the homeowner may still face a lawsuit and, ultimately, be forced to pay a judgment, but his property would not automatically be held as collateral. The lien period usually begins either on the date the work commences, or on the last day work was performed; this varies by state.

## Notice of Intent

Most states require that before filing a lien the claimant deliver a notice of Intent to Lien (or the "twenty-one day notice"[40]) to the party against whose property the lien will be filed. This gives notice to the party that there is a claim, or potential claim, against his or her property. He or she has the opportunity to resolve the claim before their property is liened. There is a minimum waiting period between notice and the actual filing of the lien.

Notices of Intent are useful to protect an owner against surprises coming from suppliers or subcontractors, and even, occasionally, from workers. An owner generally knows if he owes money to his general contractor. Resolving these two different sources of liens is slightly different.

---

[40] Check your state; various jurisdictions have different time requirements or limits.

Notices are typically required to be published in a newspaper of general circulation and to be sent by certified or registered mail to the party in jeopardy.

## Preliminary Notice

Some states, such as California, require a preliminary notice be given by the vendor to the owner, thus alerting the owner to the fact that a person has, or is about to, provide services to their project, and thus has or will have lien rights. The general contractor is exempt from this requirement because it is presumed that, since the owner signed a contract with the general contractor, he knows that the general contractor is performing work on his property.

Receipt of a preliminary notice is not cause for alarm. All experienced subcontractors and suppliers routinely file preliminary notices as a matter of course. This actually benefits the owner because then he or she can monitor his payments to the contractor and make sure that everyone who should be paid is actually getting paid. It also provides a way of verifying who is on the vendors list. Using this information you have the ability to make joint payments to the contractor and the vendor.

## Lien Waivers

A Lien Waiver is a written statement by the contractor accompanying a Payment Request stating that, upon payment of the monies owed to him for the work completed as set forth in the Payment Request, he will have been paid in full for all work performed through the effective date of the lien waiver (which should coincide with the effective date of the payment request), except for any exceptions stated in the waiver, and that, upon payment AND negotiation of the instrument of payment, he waives any claim for additional or further payment for that work AND waives his statutory or other legal rights to file a mechanic's lien against the project property. The Lien Waiver is "conditional" in that negotiation of the instrument of payment is a condition precedent to the waiver being offered by the contractor (as inducement to payment[41]).

A Lien Waiver does not preclude future claims or legal action; it simply – but very importantly – releases the property from being attached as collateral in any such future litigation or claims dispute. (It is, however, good evidence of what the contractor believed himself to be owed at the time.)

**DO NOT EVER MAKE _ANY_ PAYMENT ABSENT A SIGNED LIEN WAIVER.** You will note that this is the only advice in this entire book in bold face caps.[42]

**177**

Absent your receipt of a Lien Waiver, your contractor can file a lien against your property and, in extreme cases, force the sale of your property to collect payment on monies which are, or he claims, owed to him. A properly phrased Lien Waiver and well written contract are your best defenses in the event of a construction dispute.

A Lien Waiver should have a statement that all subcontractors and suppliers have been paid for any services or materials included in the Payment Request, or that they _will be_ paid from the proceeds of the payment. If the release is not absolute, then the Lien Waiver is a "conditional" Lien Waiver. It should also have non-conditional language certifying that all obligations represented in the previous Payment Request have been paid in full (except as

---

[41] Inducement of payment language is good to include because if your contractor makes false claims in his Schedule of Values or Payment Request, and you rely upon those claims (are induced by them) to make payment, then he has committed a fraudulent inducement which gives you further legal remedies should you need them in the event of a dispute. Fraudulent inducement may constitute a criminal offense.

[42] Not true – but I'm making a point. The other bold face capitalized advice has to do with change orders. See page 182.

disclosed).[43] I also like to include a certification that the work is fully compliant with plans, specs and codes.

## Sub-tier Lien Waivers

Not only **MUST** you obtain lien waivers from your prime (general) contractor, but you **MUST** require that he obtain lien waivers from his subcontractors and suppliers and that he provide youcopies of those waivers with his payment requests. Sub-tier waivers do not differ in form from the primary waiver. Do not disburse any monies allocable to a subcontractor or supplier without first obtaining a conditional lien waiver from that vendor. *This is critically important.* The waiver must specify through what date or for what work (work in place or materials delivered) is being waived; and, if it is for a partial payment, for what portion of the work the waiver is being made.

**178**

## Resolving Liens

| DO I NEED HELP? |
| --- |
| YES – you need a lawyer |

## Subcontractor Liens

There are several ways a subcontractor or supplier lien problem can be resolved. First, if there is no dispute that the money is owed, simply pay the bill. However no claim should taken at face value and paid without first

---

[43] A special condition of withheld monies is retainage. See page172.

investigating the circumstances. You certainly don't want to pay again if the check is already in the mail, or if the money has not been earned, or the work is defective.

---

### LIENS AS LEVERAGE

Liens, or the threat of liens, are often used as weapons in disputes between contractors and their subcontractors; or between contractors and homeowners. While liens are a concern, a lien is not a judgment or even evidence that a bill is owed or a claim is valid. It is only a means of securing collateral. Your property can sit for years with a lien on it if you have no compelling reason to remove it. Most homeowners, however, will have a mortgage lender applying pressure to remove any liens.

---

If you determine that the money is legitimately owed and you have already paid your general contractor, then you must demand that the general contractor pay the vendor immediately. Your biggest concern will be that the money you paid your contractor is no longer there.[44] Regardless of whether you have paid your contractor, your contract with him should give you the right to pay a claimant directly. Even if your contract is silent on that right, you may want to do so anyway. In either case, you will deduct that amount (which you are now paying for the second time) from money you otherwise owe your contractor.

---

[44] If that is the case, you have bigger problems.

## Protect Yourself

Be careful if you elect to pay a vendor any amount that you have already paid to your contractor. He may object to your deducting that amount from a later payment and you could then have a dispute on your hands. If you pay the vendor directly, and – say – he wasn't owed the money because your contractor fired him and hired somebody else to do the work and the subcontractor is mad and filed the lien to leverage (or extort) a settlement out of your contractor, you could be left holding the (empty) bag if you jump in and pay money which is not owed.[45] You need to advise your contractor in advance that you intend to pay the vendor directly and to hear his side of the story.

**180**

If the vendor has not completed the work to the legitimate satisfaction of the contractor, the contractor will have cause not to pay; but if he does so, he cannot bill and collect from you. Partial payments may be appropriate.

Or the subcontractor can claim that the prime contractor's basis for not paying is not legitimate and feels he must protect himself by filing a lien. Your choices: you can wait for them to work it out (which could take longer than the job lasts), you can pay the vendor yourself, or you can bond over the lien.

Bonding over a lien means that you – or better yet, your contractor[46] – deposit with the court either cash (usually one and a half times the lien amount) or a surety bond issued by an insurer licensed in the state in which the property is located. The cash or bond substitutes for the property as collateral for the claim and frees the property from the encumbrance of the lien, or threat thereof. This solution is acceptable to most lenders.

---

[45] Never mind, for the moment, that your contractor should advise you if he elects to fire or change subcontractors. If he is having trouble with a sub, he likely would not want to tell you. This is a subject that should be addressed in your construction contract.

[46] Again, have this language in your contract.

Most states prohibit specious liens – that is, the filing of a lien without just cause. If a lienor lacks just cause his lien can be dismissed and he can be sanctioned for filing a specious lien.

The worst case is that vendor liens are filed because your contractor has run out of money. This is a situation homeowners dread more than any other, and rightly so. Any vendor lien is cause for concern and should trigger an investigation. See Paying the Bills beginning on page 170. **Error! Bookmark not defined.**

## General Contractor Liens

# 181

A lien filed by your general contractor is also a serious matter. Such liens almost always result from a dispute over the value of work performed, most often extra work[47]. Or they can result when the owner runs out of funds and is unable to pay for work that he allowed to be performed.

First, if for some reason, your project funding dries up during the job – stop work immediately! Do not jeopardize what you have; if you do not stop, you could potentially lose your property.

If your contractor has performed the work, paid all his bills associated with previous payment requests, and the work is not flawed, you have no excuse not to pay him. If previous bills are not paid, you still have no cause not to pay him, but you may pay the bills unpaid from previous draws and deduct those amounts from the current payment.

If you have concerns or complaints about the work, bring them up in a timely manner. Unless you made an unlucky choice of builders, your builder

---

[47] See Change Orders beginning on page 182.

will fix whatever needs fixing. If the issue takes some time to resolve, it is not fair to withhold an entire payment – withhold a fair amount. But be sure to communicate and document what you are doing, and why. Above all, any amount withheld must be fair. You cannot withhold money earned as punishment, no matter how justified you may feel.

Most often disputes over money arise from extra work which was performed without properly executing a change order. This is a major NO-NO and the source of most construction disputes.[48] If you find yourself in this situation, try to resolve as much of the claim as you can and reduce your exposure.

# 182

## CHANGE ORDERS

---

| PUT IT IN WRITING! |
| --- |

---

Oh, how often are even experienced contractors sloppy with change orders. Change orders are a written amendment to the construction contract documenting revisions to the scope of work and setting forth the increase or decrease in the contract amount resulting therefrom. They will also document changes in the contract duration or completion date. Change orders usually have a monetary amount associated with them, but not always. For instance, if it rained for ten days straight, and the contractor couldn't work, he would submit a change order requesting ten extra days of contract time.

---

[48] The other major source of construction disputes is defective work. But that is a whole other book by itself.

## Memoranda

Some modifications to the work can be handled more informally – for instance, if the exterior paint color is red per the architect's finishes schedule and you change your mind and want blue, you can simply deliver a written memorandum (memo) to your contractor. Date it and sign it; without your signature it loses most of its value. Caution – do not assume anything to be so minor that a verbal instruction is sufficient. Although you may give the initial instruction verbally while visiting the jobsite, anything changing the expected results or altering the method of performance MUST ALWAYS be reduced to writing. And do it promptly! Also, when in doubt, go ahead and do a formal change order. Anything affecting any of the terms or conditions of the contract must be in the form of a change order.

### Initiating

Change orders may be initiated by either the owner or the contractor. An owner may decide she wants an extra window in the living room and to delete a cabinet in the laundry room. The change order would reflect an added cost to provide and install the window, and a deductive credit to delete the cabinet. The contractor would then add (or deduct) the appropriate overhead and fees. Also stated would be any change in the contract time due to the changes and a clear description of materials, styles, finishes, etc.

### Format

Owners usually insist that proposals for change orders include a high level of detail explaining any costs added or deducted, the reason being that, once your contractor is in place, you cannot go out to bid on any changes. You are dependent upon him and he should be prepared for full disclosure on changes. Your base contract should carefully spell out the terms of change orders – how much overhead and contractor's profit is allowed, what labor and equipment rates are to be, the level of cost detail to be provided, whether backup materials (such as written vendor proposals) are to be provided, and other particulars. Markups on change orders, in my opinion, should be less than fixed fee markups because change orders are negotiated and risk is reduced. Change orders should be dated and numbered sequentially.

Once signed by both parties, a change order becomes a part of the contract and is an enforceable agreement. **NEVER ALLOW ANY CHANGES TO THE PERFORMANCE OR SCOPE OF THE WORK ABSENT A WRITTEN CHANGE ORDER.**

**184**  Well drawn plans, comprehensive specifications and a clear scope of work help avoid unnecessary change orders. Ideally the only change orders on your project would come from changes you make to the design or finishes, or the scope of work itself. The reality is that every construction project encounters the unexpected. Be prepared, and have an amount of money budgeted beyond the initial contract amount for changes. A good amount would be 5% - 10% of the contract amount, depending upon the complexity of the project, the thoroughness of the plans or the extent of known issues left unresolved prior to commencing work (not usually a good idea.)

Insist that you be informed of every change that will modify or deliver the finished product in a manner, or with materials, different than set forth in the plans and specs. Remember, you are buying – and your contractor agreed to deliver – what's in the plans, not something different or similar.

## SAMPLE CHANGE ORDER

Jones Residence
123 Happy Lane
Happy Town, USA

CO # 5
June 1, 2013

That certain contract between Contractor and Owner (named below) dated March 1, 2013, is hereby modified as follows:

1. Substitute 22 gauge copper flashing for 22 galvanized flashing:

| | Qty | Unit | Rate | Extension |
|---|---|---|---|---|
| Galv flashing | (325) | LF | 2.75 | ( 893.75) |
| Copper flashing | 325 | LF | 5.15 | 1,673.75 |
| Tax | | | 8.75% | 68.25 |
| Processing fee | | | | 100.00 |
| Total Increase (Decrease) | | | | $ 948.25 |

2. There shall be no change in the completion date.
3. All other terms and conditions of the contract remain unchanged.

| | |
|---|---|
| Original Contract Amount | $ 250,000.00 |
| Previous Change Orders | 21,312.50 |
| Previous Revised Contract Amount | 271,312.50 |
| This Change Order | 948.25 |
| New Contract Amount | $272,260.75 |

So agreed on the date written above by

CONTRACTOR
Joe's Contracting

By: _____

OWNER

By: _____

By: _____

185

Attached to a change order proposal should be bids, invoices, labor time estimates and any other information appropriate or necessary for you to make an informed decision about the validity of the cost change proposed. Also, check the arithmetic.

If a change is made without your consent, do not accept it, even if it means removing and replacing the work. If you intend to consent, do so in a written change order. (If the work is already done, you may be able to negotiate a credit for accepting non-conforming work.) Do not pay for extra work that is not subject to a written change order. Your contract should provide that the contractor has no right to collect for work not authorized by you, in writing.[49]

**186**

## Emergencies

Often on the jobsite unexpected things come up that must be dealt with on the spot. If it is strictly between your contractor and one of his subcontractors, he will deal with it and it won't be of concern to you. However, if it affects the finished product, it is your concern. Make it clear that you are to be contacted *at the time* – and make yourself available to your contractor – so that any such items can be promptly resolved. Send an email or text with your instructions. Always put any instructions regarding a variance in the contracted work in writing. These written communications will be the basis for the change order. Keep current with change orders, while the subject matter is fresh in your mind.

Occasionally there will be an emergency on a job which the contractor must deal with to prevent damage or loss and there is simply no time, or he is

---

[49] If your contractor performs work without authorization and you do not feel it fair to pay, your first concern will be to not let the situation escalate out of control. Perhaps bring in your architect to mediate. Oftentimes the pain of paying a compromise amount is far less than the pain, and expense, of fighting it out. The best defense is to maintain regular – even daily – communication with contractor and to be clear and consistent with your expectations.

unable, to reach the owner. Prudence and good sense demand that the contractor take action. In that instance, the contractor should do so (the contract should require him to do so) and the owner is obligated to reimburse the contractor's out of pocket costs plus a reasonable markup.

---

### NOTHING IS FREE IN CONSTRUCTION!

Don't assume, just because he hasn't given you a bill or a change order that your contractor is performing that extra work "as a favor". Not likely. There are no "favors" in construction.

Stay on top of all changes and extra work. Nothing is more of a shock than when your contractor asks to sit down with you at the end of the job to "go over a few things". Those few things – that you thought you were getting for free – will likely add up to several thousand dollars. At this point, you have no choice. Back when he did the work you did have a choice. Pay attention, know the costs before the work happens, and maintain the discipline imposed by using change orders. Your pocketbook will thank you.

---

187

# INSURANCE

You **MUST** require that your prime contractor and each of his subcontractors maintain certain minimum insurance coverages while on the job. Your contractor is responsible for the conditions of and activities on the jobsite. If a hazard exists, he should be responsible, not you; he should be the primary party an injured or damaged party should look to, not you. You want your contractor protected by insurance so that, in a damage or loss event, compensation can be had from him. He covers himself by carrying insurance.

## General Liability Insurance

The first coverage needed is general liability insurance. General liability protects him – and you – from property or bodily injury claims due to an accident on the jobsite, or failure of the work. For instance, if the building inspector steps in hole and breaks his ankle, the contractor's liability insurance pays the medical expenses and any claims or awards for pain and suffering, or the like. It also pays for defense (attorneys' fees). Liability also pays for damages to your property or the work resulting from acts of the contractor's workers – paint overspray on your car, for instance – or failure of the work of the contractor – the new roof leaks and ruins the hardwood floor. The insurance pays the cost of replacing the hardwood floor. It does not, however, pay the cost of re-doing the defective work. That comes out of the contractor's pocket. Be sure that your contract makes that clear.

Construction liability insurance is written as "claims made" or "occurrence". The difference is significant. With claims made you are covered only if the insurance is in effect at the time the claim is made. With occurrence, you are covered if the event giving rise to the claim occurred during the term the insurance was in effect. For instance, if you purchased insurance for the period of June 1 through December 31, and a loss occurred on September 1, with a claims made policy you would only be covered if the claim was made between September 1 and December 31 – in other words, during the policy period. If you did not file the claim until the following January, you are out of luck. With an occurrence policy, you can make the claim anytime; however, if the cause occurred after December 31, you are out of luck. Require that all policies be occurrence.

Another consideration is the "tail". A tail covers warranty or defects claims for a set period *after* the expiration of the policy. This is important, because many structural warranty or water penetration claims do not arise until years later. The work occurs during the policy period, but the loss occurred after the policy period. Have your contractor obtain tail coverage if you can. Especially valuable is a ten year tail, which covers most statutory warranty periods. That way, a claim can be made for a loss which occurred during, did not become apparent until after the end of, the policy period.

189

Policies are also sometimes written on a project or location basis. There is nothing inherently wrong with this, provided it is *your* project or location which is covered by your contractor's policy. Be sure that coverage extends to workers who may be offsite but working on the project (directing traffic, driving to the landfill).

## Automobile Insurance

Next is automotive coverage. You want to be protected from any claims resulting from the use of vehicles by the contractor on site, or off site, in furtherance of your project. This is similar to your personal automobile policy. Automobile liability should cover any automobile used by your contractor on, or pursuant to, the job, including hired autos and delivery trucks. Do not accept a policy that limits auto coverage only to certain named or scheduled vehicles.

## Workers Compensation Insurance

Workers compensation insurance is required of every person or business that employs workers. Although mandated by law, that doesn't mean your contractor has it. Small, self-employed contractors are exempt if they have no employees. Many small outfits try to circumvent the law by treating employees as 1099 independent contractors (see Employees at page 158 in the Contract Terms section). Don't buy that; require workers comp even if your contractor claims not to have employees. (The only exception would be if you hire a handyman to fix your screen door.)

## 190 Builder's Risk Insurance

Builder's risk, also known as course of construction insurance, protects against fire or catastrophic loss of the partially completed improvements while they are being built and before they come under the protection of your homeowner's policy. Usually builder's risk is purchased by the owner outside of the contract. It also usually requires a monthly audit to update the value of work in place. Your payment schedule becomes a handy tool. You will need to report the delivery of any materials to the jobsite which are stored but not yet incorporated. Managing a builder's risk policy requires active attention on your part. A risk policy terminates when the improvements are placed in service, at which time your homeowner's policy will insure against loss.

## Coverages

Typical insurance and amounts of coverage you need to require of your contractor are

| | |
|---|---|
| General Liability | $1,000,000 for each occurrence |
| | $1,000,000 personal and bodily injury |
| | $1,000,000 products and completed operations (aggregate) |
| | $1,000,000 general aggregate[50] |
| Automobile Liability | $500,000 combined single limit each accident |
| | $300,000 bodily injury each person |
| | $300,000 bodily injury per accident |
| | $300,000 property damage per accident |
| Umbrella | the more the better; $2 - $5,000,000 is the usual range[51] |

191

---

[50] Try for $2,000,000 general aggregate.

[51] Sometimes less is better. If the pot of gold (in insurance money) small or not there, a lawsuit may not be attractive to the (allegedly) injured party (or a potential lawyer).

Worker's Compensation                    the requirements are usually set by
                                          state law

Be sure your insurance requirements are spelled out in your general contract before starting the job, including the requirement that insurance be maintained at all times during the contract term and whenever the contractor, his agents or his hires are on the job. Also require that you be given thirty days written notice prior to the cancellation of the policy(ies) for any reason. You will also want the right to pay the insurance premiums yourself upon receipt of a notice of cancellation for non-payment.[52] Any such payments should be deductible from monies otherwise payable to the contractor.

**192**

Lenders' will often require that risk payments be made to them once they have advanced money. Also be sure that your policies provide for debris removal and cleanup and includes an escalator (replacement cost) clause. Most loss policies will exclude the foundation, but try to argue that; you likely won't win, but you can try.

## Subcontractor Requirements

The prime contract should require that all subcontractors carry policies of insurance equal to or better than required of the general contractor. In practice, this may be harder to obtain, especially from small contractors, particularly for the amounts of liability coverage and the umbrella. You may elect to accept a $500,000 aggregate and occurrence limit for certain small contractors with a limited risk profile; and to waive the umbrella. Never take less than $1,000,000 from the prime contractor.

---

[52] Non payment of insurance premiums is a huge red flag. You should be immediately concerned about your contractor's financial viability and take reasonable steps to protect yourself. In extreme cases this may mean cancelling the contract. Be sure the contract gives you this remedy.

Most insurance policies will exclude liability for hazardous waste, contaminated soils, asbestos, mold, radio-activity, war, riot, terrorism, unstable soils and certain other hazards. You may obtain these coverages, but they will be expensive.

### INSURANCE DISCLAIMER

- Consult an insurance broker with experience writing construction related policies; your homeowner's agent may lack the expertise to properly advise you.

- The guidelines discussed here are ony that; consult an expert.

193

## Certificate of Insurance

A certificate of insurance is a one page summary of the insurance carried by a policy holder. It will be issued by the policy holder's producer (agent) and will list the insurance carried, the issuing insurers, each policy number, the term of each policy and the limits. It will have the date the certificate was issued and it will be signed by an authorized representative. Always, always demand an original with a wet signature. Signature stamps are often used. I don't like them, but it may not be worth the argument

**194**

The certificate will be made out to a certificate holder; that is you. In addition, require that any certificate of insurance state that you are an "additional insured." Being the certificate holder only means that you are being informed of the insurance; being an additional insured means that you are actually covered as well as the policy holder. This is very important. Language to that effect should be included in the insurance section of the prime contract. Check the certificate to confirm that the square next to the policy type for additional insured is checked or that there is a statement entered in one of the boxes at the bottom of the certificate set forth the names of any additional insureds you have requested. If there is a lender they will also demand a certificate of insurance and to be named as an additional insured. Collect certificates of insurance from all subcontractors; have certificates in your possession before you allow any contractor or subcontractor onto the jobsite.

Require that the certificate of insurance be issued on ACORD form 25 (2010/05).

ACORD

# CERTIFICATE OF LIABILITY INSURANCE

DATE (MM/DD/YYYY)

THIS CERTIFICATE IS ISSUED AS A MATTER OF INFORMATION ONLY AND CONFERS NO RIGHTS UPON THE CERTIFICATE HOLDER. THIS CERTIFICATE DOES NOT AFFIRMATIVELY OR NEGATIVELY AMEND, EXTEND OR ALTER THE COVERAGE AFFORDED BY THE POLICIES BELOW. THIS CERTIFICATE OF INSURANCE DOES NOT CONSTITUTE A CONTRACT BETWEEN THE ISSUING INSURER(S), AUTHORIZED REPRESENTATIVE OR PRODUCER, AND THE CERTIFICATE HOLDER.

IMPORTANT: If the certificate holder is an ADDITIONAL INSURED, the policy(ies) must be endorsed. If SUBROGATION IS WAIVED, subject to the terms and conditions of the policy, certain policies may require an endorsement. A statement on this certificate does not confer rights to the certificate holder in lieu of such endorsement(s).

| | | |
|---|---|---|
| PRODUCER | CONTACT NAME: | |
| | PHONE (A/C, No, Ext): | FAX (A/C, No): |
| | E-MAIL ADDRESS: | |
| | INSURER(S) AFFORDING COVERAGE | NAIC # |
| | INSURER A : | |
| INSURED | INSURER B : | |
| | INSURER C : | |
| | INSURER D : | |
| | INSURER E : | |
| | INSURER F : | |

COVERAGES CERTIFICATE NUMBER: REVISION NUMBER:

THIS IS TO CERTIFY THAT THE POLICIES OF INSURANCE LISTED BELOW HAVE BEEN ISSUED TO THE INSURED NAMED ABOVE FOR THE POLICY PERIOD INDICATED. NOTWITHSTANDING ANY REQUIREMENT, TERM OR CONDITION OF ANY CONTRACT OR OTHER DOCUMENT WITH RESPECT TO WHICH THIS CERTIFICATE MAY BE ISSUED OR MAY PERTAIN, THE INSURANCE AFFORDED BY THE POLICIES DESCRIBED HEREIN IS SUBJECT TO ALL THE TERMS, EXCLUSIONS AND CONDITIONS OF SUCH POLICIES. LIMITS SHOWN MAY HAVE BEEN REDUCED BY PAID CLAIMS.

| INSR LTR | TYPE OF INSURANCE | ADDL INSR | SUBR WVD | POLICY NUMBER | POLICY EFF (MM/DD/YYYY) | POLICY EXP (MM/DD/YYYY) | LIMITS | |
|---|---|---|---|---|---|---|---|---|
| | GENERAL LIABILITY<br>COMMERCIAL GENERAL LIABILITY<br>CLAIMS-MADE OCCUR<br>GEN'L AGGREGATE LIMIT APPLIES PER:<br>POLICY PRO-JECT LOC | | | | | | EACH OCCURRENCE | $ |
| | | | | | | | DAMAGE TO RENTED PREMISES (Ea occurrence) | $ |
| | | | | | | | MED EXP (Any one person) | $ |
| | | | | | | | PERSONAL & ADV INJURY | $ |
| | | | | | | | GENERAL AGGREGATE | $ |
| | | | | | | | PRODUCTS - COMP/OP AGG | $ |
| | | | | | | | | $ |
| | AUTOMOBILE LIABILITY<br>ANY AUTO<br>ALL OWNED AUTOS SCHEDULED AUTOS<br>HIRED AUTOS NON-OWNED AUTOS | | | | | | COMBINED SINGLE LIMIT (Ea accident) | $ |
| | | | | | | | BODILY INJURY (Per person) | $ |
| | | | | | | | BODILY INJURY (Per accident) | $ |
| | | | | | | | PROPERTY DAMAGE (Per accident) | $ |
| | | | | | | | | $ |
| | UMBRELLA LIAB OCCUR<br>EXCESS LIAB CLAIMS-MADE<br>DED RETENTION $ | | | | | | EACH OCCURRENCE | $ |
| | | | | | | | AGGREGATE | $ |
| | | | | | | | | $ |
| | WORKERS COMPENSATION AND EMPLOYERS' LIABILITY Y / N<br>ANY PROPRIETOR/PARTNER/EXECUTIVE OFFICER/MEMBER EXCLUDED? (Mandatory in NH)<br>If yes, describe under DESCRIPTION OF OPERATIONS below | N / A | | | | | WC STATU-TORY LIMITS OTH-ER | |
| | | | | | | | E.L. EACH ACCIDENT | $ |
| | | | | | | | E.L. DISEASE - EA EMPLOYEE | $ |
| | | | | | | | E.L. DISEASE - POLICY LIMIT | $ |

DESCRIPTION OF OPERATIONS / LOCATIONS / VEHICLES (Attach ACORD 101, Additional Remarks Schedule, if more space is required)

| CERTIFICATE HOLDER | CANCELLATION |
|---|---|
| | SHOULD ANY OF THE ABOVE DESCRIBED POLICIES BE CANCELLED BEFORE THE EXPIRATION DATE THEREOF, NOTICE WILL BE DELIVERED IN ACCORDANCE WITH THE POLICY PROVISIONS. |
| | AUTHORIZED REPRESENTATIVE |



ACORD 25 (2010/05)



**Figure 12: Acord From 25**

195

# the jobsite

Finally, we get to start work. In this final section we will look at the tools and procedures used by successful contractors to manage their projects. Good communication among all the parties is a common thread of all successful projects, as well as good record keeping. Also important is the deportment of the job and the workers. We look at how to assure quality in the work and what constitutes completion.

The last thing we look at is dispute resolution. Not really a part of the job, but disputes, when they occur, most often arise out of defects in the work, verbal instructions or extra work. We look at how to avoid disputes, and what to do when they do occur.

199

## THE SCHEDULE AND SCHEDULING

Although the project schedule should be addressed as early as the bid documents – bidders are often asked to provide an estimated time to complete the project as part of their bid proposals – and most definitely should be addressed in the contract documents – usually as a completion deadline – it really becomes central to the project during the construction phase. While the plans show what is to be delivered, the schedule controls when it is to be delivered. Thus the schedule becomes key to the entire successful execution of the project.

Construction schedules can be as simple as a sequential list of tasks to be accomplished; or as complicated as a cross-word puzzle. Typically used is the bar chart schedule, which is a vertical presentation listing tasks in their order of performance and the time allocated to each, represented as a horizontal bar. A timeline or calendar is scheduled across the top. Each task can be further broken down to greater levels of detail.

**200**

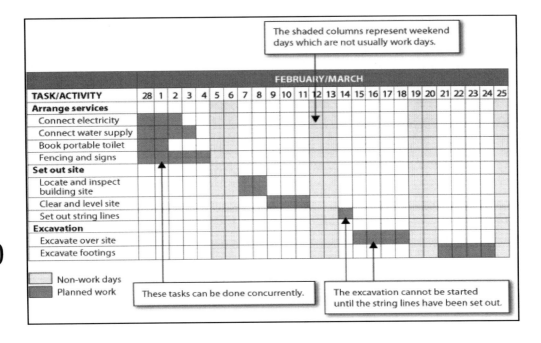

Figure 13: Sample of a simple construction schedule in bar chart format.

A simple bar chart, such as that shown in Figure 14, gives the project manager the ability to visualize and plan for upcoming activities. Actual progress can be followed by re-coloring task bars as work is completed and with a moving vertical line showing the actual date versus the predicted date. This allows a quick understanding of the progress of a job.

More sophisticated charts will color code the time bars to show critical path items – those tasks which must be completed before a subsequent task can be started – versus non-critical path items, which are items upon which no subsequent task is dependent. The progress of a project revolves around the ability of the superintendent to keep the critical path items on schedule. Figure 15 shows task bars color coded and with arrows linking the predecessor task to the dependent task. Notice that some tasks may be accomplished in parallel, while others are strictly sequential. It is your contractor's ability to orchestrate actual performance to match scheduled performance that allows him to bring your project in on time.

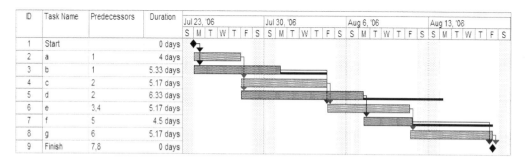

**Figure 14: Gantt chart with critical path indicators.**

201

These types of scheduling charts are called Gantt Charts, named after Henry Gantt who first developed the methodology in 1910. Gantt charting can range from the very simple, to complex presentations tracking time, expenditures, conditions and all types of information pertinent to the production of work. Most residential charts stay on the simple side.

Schedules are often optimistic and are subject to frequent revision. Try to be realistic with original schedule. Listen to your contractor when he says how long it will take and make that, not what you wish it would be, the basis of your schedule to avoid frustration during the project.

# COMMUNICATING

I cannot over-emphasize the value of clear, consistent communication during a construction project.  Not only will it facilitate timely completion, but it will prevent oversights and errors and is the single most important tool to prevent disputes.    Troubled  jobs  are  invariably  plagued  with  poor communications;  managers  of  successful  jobs  are  invariably  excellent communicators.

The communication starts with well-crafted construction documents, a fair  and  balanced  contract  and  continues  through  the  term  of  the  job. Experienced managers rely upon telephones, email, written memos and even letters.  Communication is constant and flows in all directions, back and forth. An involved owner will be involved in the flow of information on his or her project.

An important aspect of successful communication is respect for the chain of command.  It is disruptive for an owner to give directions, for instance, to the tile setter working for the tile subcontractor working for the general contractor working for the owner.  Yes, the tile setter is ultimately working for you; and yes, it is your project – but if you go outside the chain of command, you are undermining the successful flow of information, and confusing the various subsidiary parties.  Conflicting instructions create confusion; confusion creates mistakes and errors; mistakes and errors cost money...and we know who will ultimately be asked to pay.

While verbal resolution of issues is faster and usually more productive than  written  exchanges,  *always*  reduce  decisions  to  writing.  Sign  your instructions to your contractor and have him acknowledge receipt.  Before texting and emails we used double carbon memos – write the memo, sign it, keep one copy, send two to the other party, he or she replies, signs and returns one.  Now you each have a written record.  It's a great system.  If you rely upon

202

email, be sure to collect acknowledgements, even if it requires nagging the other party.  If necessary, send a letter on important matters.

Always keep your cool on the jobsite and in meetings with your contractor.  If you are a husband and wife, as is likely, be sure you are on the same page.  You can't have one spouse giving one instruction and other some contradictory instruction.  Above all, even though it is your house and you may get stressed or emotional at times, keep it professional.

## Pre Construction Meeting

Every project should start with a kick off or pre-construction (the "pre-con") meeting attended by all the major participants in the project.  They are the onsite superintendent, the owner, the owner's rep (if any), the project manager[53] (if different than the superintendent), the architect (if one is involved), building manager (if applicable) and the major subcontractors.

**203**

At the pre-con meeting you will go over the lines of communication, jobsite rules, performance expectations, access and parking issues, material storage, dumpster and toilet location, schedule, change order procedure, RFI procedure, jobsite safety, visitors, cleanup and any other issues pertinent to the project.  I recommend having the contractor lead the meeting; after all, it is his job.  He should be seen by all parties as clearly in charge of the jobsite.

One important purpose of the initial meeting is to have all the participants meet each other and to give each, especially the subcontractors, the

---

[53] On larger projects, such as a new home, the superintendent will usually be dedicated full time to the project; on smaller remodel projects, the superintendent may be supervising several jobs.  In either case, with larger companies the company owner may, but likely will not, attend this meeting.  Remember, he or she is running an entire company with multiple other projects and many responsibilities.  If you are not comfortable unless the owner attends, by all means ask him or her to do so.

opportunity to ask questions and to voice any concerns they may have about the schedule, the execution of their work or special needs they may have. The idea is to establish a harmonious team for a successful project. Everyone should exchange cell phone numbers and email addresses.

One rule to insist upon is that the superintendent always answer his calls, or return them immediately. Simply put – no delay in response is acceptable. But, in exchange for this commitment, don't abuse it. Respect your supervisor's private time and don't waste his time with trivialities or emergencies that aren't. Try to consolidate your questions (often times they will answer themselves) for one call or meeting. Also, you in return must be available to him or the project manager. If you are unavailable when they need a decision or direction it can disrupt or delay the project. Keep in mind: they cannot make your decisions for you.

## Weekly Meetings

On larger jobs there should be a meeting once a week attended by the superintendent, the project manager and the architect (if any), and the owner. It may also be appropriate to have one or more subcontractors whose work may currently be ongoing. This is your opportunity to bring up your accrued questions, request changes or raise any other issues or concerns you may have. And their opportunity to address their issues needing your attention.

The project manager or superintendent should convey an updated schedule, present any decisions which must be made by the owner, update the general progress of the work and raise any other matters of concern. The architect will have the opportunity to walk the job and to review the compliance and quality of the work.

## Project Visits

Visit your project often. Take lots of pictures. Keep a diary.

Project visits keep you informed. They give you the chance to see the progress of the work, take note of manpower levels and jobsite conditions, and to chat with the workers. (Remember, unless you are an owner builder directly hiring workers, they work for their boss, not directly for you. While it is perfectly permissible to chat with them, you need to respect the chain of command. Don't give them instructions directly – this only confuses communications, irritates the superintendent, leads to misunderstandings, leaves your contractor uninformed and usually ends up costing you money.)

**205**

When you visit your jobsite, whether it's a new house or the next room, try not to interrupt or disrupt the workers – basically, stay out of the way and let them do their jobs. If you see something you don't like or are uncertain of, bring it to the attention of the project superintendent or your contractor.

Pictures and your diary are a permanent record of the progress of the job. While a diary can be colored by personal opinion or bias, pictures speak for themselves. In the event of a dispute, both are invaluable. Hopefully there will be no dispute, and the pictures go into a scrapbook which you will occasionally flip through in later years and trigger a memory or a chuckle.

Don't be shy about taking pictures; after all, it is your property and your project. You have every right to do so, and the contractor has no legitimate objection to your doing so. A good time to visit jobs is in the late afternoon or early evening after the workers have left. This gives you the opportunity to quietly contemplate – and enjoy the progress of – your project without interruption or distractions; you can poke around to your heart's content.

Get in the habit of writing down a recap of all phone calls or conversations in your diary as soon as possible after having them. Contemporaneous notes are very powerful evidence in the event of a misunderstanding or dispute. Good notes can refresh everyone's memory and prevent misunderstandings from escalating. Just the succinct points is enough; no need to recount every word verbatim.

## Jobsite Records

Larger projects should have a field office. Properly this should be different than a tool storage shed. A good field office will have a desk, plans table, computer and printer/copier/fax, and a file drawer. We used to have a telephone, but anymore the superintendent will be working from his cell phone. Your superintendent should keep a copy of every project document *in his file*. Note the italics. Just as the jobsite should be neat, so should the field office. The tone of the job rests with the superintendent; the organization of his office will tell you a lot.

Examples of jobsite records are materials delivery tickets, requests for information and the responses, change requests and proposals, architect and owner correspondence, the building permit and the approved set of plans, the safety plan and any accident reports.

A good superintendent will keep a daily log which records the weather, trades on the job and manpower levels, work pursued during the day, jobsite visits, verbal instructions – either given or received – and any other event or information pertaining to the job. Although his diary is not something you can expect access to, you have the right to view any other project document.

I also recommend keeping a box of double carbon memos on the job. They are ideal for documenting jobsite questions, answers and instructions.

## Requests for Information

A Request for Information (or RFI) is initiated by the contractor or one of his subcontractors. They usually involve clarifications of or questions as to the intent of the drawings. RFIs are usually answered by a written memo from the architect, or a sketch. RFIs should be numbered consecutively and dated; response memos should be dated and refer to the RFI number. Sketches should also be dated and numbered, and referenced to the plans page or detail as appropriate. Sketches typically are numbered SK-1, etc.

RFIs may lead to change orders, but often they – and the response memo or sketch – stand alone. Requests for information, and the answers, do become part of the project record.

**207**

## Materials Selections

One frequent obstacle to the timely progress of work on a project is the selection of finishes, colors, fixtures and appliances by the owner. While it may seem that selecting the kitchen sink or the refrigerator may not be urgent while a project is at bare studs, it may in fact be critical. Framing must be sized to accommodate what comes later, including windows, doors and refrigerators. Special items may involve long lead times.

The builder will have a list of selections to be made or confirmed by the homeowner. Each selection should be individually initialed to avoid any misunderstanding. Then the contractor will be confident to move forward. The contractor may also submit products or materials for approval. These submittals may include technical specifications which need to be reviewed for consistency with the owner's or architect's intent. The owner or architect will keep the job moving along by promptly reviewing and approving (or asking for a re-submittal) of submittals.

Other items are often provided to the contractor by the homeowner for installation. It is important that the contractor communicates a deadline to the homeowner for selections and for delivery of owner provided items and that the homeowner respects the deadline. It is not fair to blame a contractor for delays which are actually lack of performance by the homeowner. Remember, the contractor is at a disadvantage; since he is working for you he has no leverage to force your timely performance.

Items most often supplied by homeowners are light fixtures, appliances, door knobs, cabinet pulls, and plumbing fixtures. With all owner supplied materials, be clear on who is responsible for delivery; and whether delivery means curbside, unloaded to the driveway, or in the house. With plumbing fixtures care must be taken to define who is to supply connecting parts. With appliances, be clear who is to uncrate them and who is to install them.

**208**

## HOUSEKEEPING

I can't over-emphasize good housekeeping on a jobsite. Insist that your project be kept clean. That means, not just once in a while, or even at the end of the workday, but continuously while work is being performed. All scrap and debris should be disposed of as it is generated. There should never be debris underfoot, piles of trash, lunch wrappers or soda cans tossed about. Absolutely no smoking should be allowed inside. (I don't even like it outside.)

Projects should be kept broom clean at all times. This is especially important for remodel jobs where the work is being performed inside an existing home – usually while the owners continue to live there. For remodel projects the work areas should be isolated from the rest of the house by plastic barriers taped into place. There should be zipper doors for access, if direct outside access is not available. Remodel projects should be vacuumed daily.

Particular care must be given to dust control, especially during drywall sanding. Ask for a dust control plan (this should be addressed in the contract).

Your contractor should provide trash cans, brooms and shop vacuums on the project.

Designate an area for material storage, the dumpster and the portable toilet; also how often the toilet is to be serviced. Your contract should address protection of and damage to lawns and plants. Will the irrigation system be turned off, and will special watering be required?

> A clean workplace promotes clean work.

## QUALITY CONTROL

Quality control begins before the work is started. It begins with a quality set of plans and specifications. The plans should leave no question as to what is intended and how it is to be constructed. Well-written specifications will clearly define materials (and grades) to be used, how the work is to be assembled and tolerances for the work. For instance, for painting not only would the brand[54] and ASTM[55] reference be set forth, but the requirements for surface preparation, number of coats to be applied, tinting variations between coats, method of application (for instance spray or brush) and curing time between coats.

---

[54] Often the phrase "or equal" is used. That works fine for some items, but you may be very particular about others – such as the appliances.

[55] American Society for Testing and Materials.

Before any stage of work is commenced – say pouring a concrete patio – it is wise to review the specifications and the performance standards, especially when finished surfaces are involved. Review the planned method of execution with your contractor; make sure the number of workers he plans to use is adequate[56]; check the travel time from the batch plant; ask how the reinforcing mersh is to be lifted, etc. Achieving quality consists of anticipating, planning for and executing numerous small and large steps. It is difficult to replace experience when it comes to assuring quality execution of construction work.

**210**

For field finished surfaces (drywall, concrete, plaster, paint colors) you should require that your contractor prepare a sample for your approval. The sample should be not less than 3' x 3'. For factory prepared finishes or materials (carpet, wood flooring, cabinets) have your contractor submit a sample (this is called a submittal) for your review and approval before he orders and installs it.

The easiest form of quality control is to hire an experienced and conscientious contractor. Even then it is important to keep an eye on things. Quality is usually in direct relationship to the price you pay, although paying a lot and getting poor quality is unfortunately not unknown. Rarely will you pay the least and get good quality.

---

### THE RULE OF TIME, PRICE & QUALITY

To achieve high quality and be done quickly, you will pay a high price;

To achieve high quality at a low price, you will sacrifice time;

To have a low price and be done quickly, you will sacrifice quality.

---

[56] Very important with concrete; if the number of workers is inadequate, the concrete may not be dispersed within the delivery time set in the specs or the crew may be too short-handed to properly finish the surface before it hardens.

Quality work requires quality materials. Spend time during the planning stage with your architect to ensure that your specifications call for the type and quality of materials you are expecting. But you must also be willing to pay for those materials; better materials always cost more than inferior materials. An early clue can be found in the bid results: if a bidder is way lower than the other bidders, it could well be that he has priced lesser quality materials (or he just made a mistake; either way, you don't want him). Especially compare the pricing between bidders for the finishes.

Quality is also a function of the skill of the workers. Skill comes with experience, and experience demands – and deserves – more money. Be sure when you are buying contracting services that you are clear about the level of skill that a contractor is offering you.

**211**

Finally, quality is a factor of the haste with which a job performed. Good work takes time. There is a difference between hasty and fast. A job can be run fast if it is well planned and executed, reasonable amounts of time are allowed for tasks, and time is not wasted through lack of competent scheduling. Haste is running around because things are disorganized and time is running out. No fine craftsmanship is ever achieved in haste.

One way to avoid haste is to hire an experienced contractor. Also important is to pay enough for the work desired. When a vendor is not receiving an adequate and fair amount of money he is going to push his workers to produce faster. This almost always yields a poorer quality of work. The result to the owner is unhappiness with the finished product or extra expense to remove and redo the work, ultimately costing you more than if you had paid the right price to begin with. A provider under financial pressure may also substitute cheaper materials.[57]

---

[57] It is very important that your plans and specifications clearly specify and describe the products and materials to be incorporated into the work.

Be ready to pay for the materials you want; likewise, be ready to pay for the craftsmanship you want.

Keep your job site clean. This is one of the simplest ways to improve the quality of the work. It not only creates an easier work area to function in, but it also engenders an atmosphere of respect for the project.

Also realize that jobs lacking in adequate and experienced supervision are prone to errors, omissions, shortcuts and sloppy work. One of the most common mistakes inexperienced buyers of building services want to make is to try and save money by reducing supervision. Reducing supervision will **ALWAYS** lead to mistakes, delays and poor quality. Lack of supervision will cost you far more – *every time* – than any apparent savings.

212

> Saving money on supervision is the most expensive money you never save.

Walk your project frequently to observe the work. Watch how it is being performed; observe the workers to see if they seem attentive and competent. Observe the workplace – is it organized and the clean? Don't be intimidated; ask questions and feel free to challenge the answers. Ask to borrow a level and check things for level, plumb and square. Listen to your gut; if something doesn't seem right (doesn't pass the smell test) ask for an explanation. If you are in doubt, feel free to have work stopped until you are satisfied. [58] Seek outside advice if you feel you need to. Remember, you are the one writing the checks.

---

[58] Caution: try not to make a habit of stopping work. If you are that concerned about what's going on, it's time to hire a professional owner's representative. Continually stopping or interfering in the progress of the work will irritate your contractor and cost him money.

# INSPECTIONS

## The Building Inspector

The building inspector is your point of contact with the building bureaucracy. Like any bureaucracy, the building department has procedures and ways of doing things. It is always good to cultivate a cordial relationship with the building inspector – he or she can help you through rough spots, or make your life very, very difficult. You do have the right to expect civility, professionalism and courtesy from your inspector.

The first and best way to create a positive relationship with the inspector is to do things right – that is, build per plans and code; don't try to cut any corners. Don't start absent a permit. Probably just as important is to "be ready" when the inspector is on the job. Usually the inspector will only visit your job when you call for an inspection. Have the plans, permit and specifications ready, clean and available.[59] The permit may include a separate inspection sign-off card. Often the building department (or the fire department) will require that the street address be posted in front of the project. Assume that the inspector wants the plans conveniently located; he will not want to hunt for them.

**213**

It is a good idea to be present when an inspection is scheduled. This can usually be narrowed to morning or afternoon; occasionally you might get a

---

Eventually he will demand compensation for extra supervision and overhead expense. Get the help you need to make informed decisions rather than let a situation get out of hand due to inexperience or uncertainty.

[59] The best way to keep plans on the jobsite is to get a piece of 3" diameter PVC plastic pipe, seal one end and put a cap on the other end, and keep the plans inside. Get a large sized zip-lock bag and place the permit inside. If you have a job sign, attach both to the job sign.

narrower window, but don't count on it. Anymore, most building departments have an automatic call-in system for scheduling inspections.

The best technique for handling an inspection is to follow the inspector around and answer any questions he has. Casual chit-chat is OK, but don't try to explain anything to him. It is usually a point of pride with an inspector that they know what they are looking at; besides, he does this all day, every day, and almost certainly knows way more about the building code than you ever will.

If he or she objects to something, ask for an explanation and get clarity on what he expects as a solution. Rarely is it good advice to argue (no matter how arrogant he may be or irritated he makes you). Find out what he wants and just do it, even if not strictly required. Even if not required by the plans, he may be asking for something required by code; all plans approvals have a catchall that requires all construction to be per code, even if the plans don't show it that way. Be aware that most building inspectors seem to have pet topics that they hone in on.

If you believe your inspector is totally out of line, or his behavior is unacceptable, then approach his superior. But be absolutely courteous and professional if you do so. Have your ducks in a row; research your argument and be sure you are on solid ground. If it is a behavior issue, have notes with dates and times of inappropriate behavior. This is tricky, but sometimes necessary.

Most building departments regularly rotate their inspectors; it is entirely possible that each inspection you call for may be by a different inspector. This can create problems on a complex project when you have been working closely with an inspector to craft solutions to various problems and you suddenly loose the continuity of that working relationship. On the other hand, if it has been a tenuous relationship, you may welcome the change.

Departments rotate inspectors to eliminate the possibility of bribes or other inappropriate behavior.[60]

All in all, building inspectors are well educated in code issues and generally I find them professional in their approach to their jobs. You will normally have only four or five inspections during the course of a job and ultimately it is your responsibility to ensure that your project is built per plans and code.

## Special Inspections

The building inspector is a specialist in building code compliance. Other types of inspections call for special knowledge or education – such as inspecting for conformance with the engineering requirements of a building. Some operations, such as the placement of concrete or gluing operations require observation during execution. These inspections and observations are typically conducted by licensed engineers, who are known as "special inspectors". The inspections are special inspections. The engineering plans will normally have a schedule of special inspections required. You must arrange for these special inspections and pay the cost of the special inspectors. Who pays is a matter that must be set forth in the scope of work attached to the general contract. If not included in the contractor's scope of work, the expense of special inspectors is only paid by the general contractor if the inspection fails. The expense of inspections is otherwise paid for by the owner.

**215**

---

[60] Although I have never had an inspector ask me for a bribe, I have had union agents "ask".

# SAFETY

> There's always time to bend a nail.

## The Safety Plan

Every project, no matter how small, should have a safety plan. In my opinion the most important safety item on a jobsite is fall protection. This means safety rails at all openings and stairways. Stairway protection is one of the most ignored – and dangerous – safety situations I have observed in over 40 years on construction jobsites. It scares me every time. Do not accept the excuse (and I can't tell you how many times I have heard this one) that "we're going to put up a rail as soon as we're finished here." What?! Think about that for a second. Isn't the purpose of the rail to provide safety *while* you're there?

---

### SAFETY RAILS

Workers like to ignore safety rails. I can't tell you how many times I've seen safety rails knocked down so that some task could be more conveniently done. Rarely do they go back up.

Many is the time I've walked onto a subfloor while the framers are framing walls only to see a stair well opening without a safety rail around it. This is basically a large hole in the floor with nothing stopping a person from just stepping through and falling to the floor or concrete slab below. "Where's your safety rail?" I'll ask. "Oh, we're going to put it up as soon as we're finished here." Whoa, hang on. Isn't the point to have protection *while* you are working?

Finally, safety rails should be constructed with same care and craftsmanship as the permanent construction. In simplest terms, a guardrail must resist the force of 200 pounds.

In my opinion, lack of adequate guardrails is the most significant safety failure on every residential jobsite.

---

There are a number of other what I would call "level 1" safety issues including excavation shoring, saw guards, electrical grounding, dust inhalation, debris, and nails sticking out of boards. And hardhats (a constant battle; frankly, hardhats are rare on residential jobs). Include the requirement for a safety plan in the contract with your builder and have penalties for failure to maintain the plan. There should always be a first aid kit on the jobsite.[61] Is there a pool; are there small children, pets? What steps should you and your contractor take to protect children and pets

---

[61] First aid kits tend to become depleted. Check to be sure it is maintained. There are services which will do so.

---

**A FEW QUICK SAFETY TIPS WHEN VISITING YOUR JOBSITE**

- Always wear shoes on the jobsite.

- When walking between studs always look up before stepping through to avoid smacking your head on a cross-block.

- If you know better, don't do it.

- Stay alert.

---

**218**

Having a safety manual on site, maintaining safety rails and keeping the jobsite clean and clear of debris will go a long ways toward minimizing any adverse impact from an OSHA inspection.[62]

## Jobsite Behavior

Include provisions in your contract to protect against unruly behavior by workers on the jobsite. Examples of undesirable behavior include profanity, drinking, smoking, drug use, being under the influence of drugs or hung-over, loud radios or music, failure to follow safety protocols, failure to keep the work area clean. Include hanging out in the street in front of the project after work (drinking beer). To me, that's a real no-no. Have parking rules.

Insisting upon good behavior engenders respect for the job, and for you. Respect for the job will result in better work.

---

[62] Occupational Safety and Health Administration. This is a federal agency; most states have similar agencies.

> Don't be afraid to walk onto your jobsite and pull the plug
> on a loud radio.  I do it all the time.

## Sanitary Facilities

As a homeowner, you do not want workers using your bathroom. Require that a portable toilet be provided, even for the shortest jobs.

# DISPUTE RESOLUTION                              219

Unfortunately disputes are not uncommon in construction. Construction projects usually involve one party hiring another party to create something that does not exist, nor has ever existed.  It depends upon drawings on paper to convey the idea of one person (the client) to the other person (the builder) in a sufficiently clear manner that the result meets the first person's expectations.

But colors chosen from chips appear different when painted on whole walls; windows aren't quite in the right place for the view; the kitchen isn't as big as anticipated.  All of this can, and does, happen.

Nor has this building or renovation ever been built before.  Nobody can be precisely sure what it will cost at the end of the day, nor exactly how long it will take.

Changes may be needed in the work – the roof plan as drawn doesn't work; the soils turn out not to be stable and expensive caissons need to be installed.  Should there have been soils borings before designing or bidding the job?  Who should have been responsible?  What do the various construction and contract documents say?  Whose fault is this oversight and who pays?

There have been delays in the job, which is now four months behind schedule.  Has the contractor been negligent with his scheduling management, or does he have legitimate claims for time extensions due to weather, homeowner indecision or due to revisions by the architect?  You are incurring extra interest on your construction loan, yet the contractor is asking for extra overhead and compensation for extended supervision.  Who's right?

**220**

One day your contractor comes to you with several change orders adding up to thousands of dollars.  You are stunned; you thought that all those "little" things you asked if he could do were favors – just part of the job.  Little did you understand that, although your builder was willing to do as you asked, he expected to get paid for it.

Six months after you move in you notice a crack in the wall; investigating you discover that the foundation has settled.  You call your contractor and, while sympathetic, he denies liability because he built per plans.  So you call the structural engineer; he passes the buck to the soils engineer.  The soils engineer stands by his report and points the finger back at the structural engineer.  To compound things, the initial soils report was ordered by you, and you have no idea how to read a soils report.  Meanwhile that crack in the wall keeps getting bigger.  Nobody wants this liability, but you're absolutely sure it's not your fault.

So what do you do?  Do you hire a lawyer ($225/hour ; $1,800/ day; $9,000/ week) and sue your builder, the soils engineer, your architect?  Or all of them.  Definitely an unhappy situation and a tough decision.

Try to resolve misunderstandings while they are little; try to avoid escalation into full blown disputes.  First try to reach a reasonable accommodation between the parties. Try to be flexible; it is helpful to try to see the problem from the other person's perspective. Be ready to give a little more than you want, and hopefully they will take the same approach. Remember, they are probably as sure of being right as you are.

---

### AVOIDING DISPUTES

The best dispute resolution is to avoid disputes in the first place. Disputes can be most easily avoided by following the simple rules and advice set forth in this book:

1. Plan carefully
2. Prepare clear and thorough plans and specifications
3. Conduct a disciplined bid
4. Choose a reputable contractor
5. Have detailed and tested contract documents
6. Expect to pay for all changes
7. Put everything in writing
8. Keep copies
9. Make a photographic record
10. Keep a diary
11. Don't ignore warning signs
12. Don't cut corners

---

221

## Mediation

If you absolutely cannot work out a disagreement directly and it escalates into a dispute, you need to turn to the dispute resolution language in your contract. Most contracts will first call for mediation. In mediation the parties to a dispute present their positions to a neutral mediator (whom they have mutually agreed to[63]) who will then practice shuttle diplomacy between the two. Don't expect the mediator to be your advocate; instead he or she will

---

[63] Assuming they can agree. The contract should provide a method of choosing a mediator, or arbitrator, when the disputing parties cannot agree upon one.

usually beat you up. He or she will point out the strengths of the other party's position, the weaknesses of yours, and the uncertainty of success should you escalate to arbitration or litigation. He knows that a settlement can only be reached if each party concedes a little. At this point you must choose whether going away a little unhappy, but problem put behind you, is better than chancing litigation. (Also, it's possible that you might realize you were not completely right or free of blame – can't tell you how many times *that's* the case.) With luck, the other party comes to the same conclusion and you settle. A mediator can only recommend and urge; a mediator cannot compel a settlement.

## 222  Arbitration

Should mediation fail, the next step is either arbitration or litigation. A arbitrator can compel a settlement. Although arbitration has been very popular, some contractors prefer litigation to arbitration. You need to make the decision about how to resolve intransigent disputes when you draft your contracts. Here are the conventional pros and cons to arbitration versus litigation:

### Speed

Arbitration is usually faster than litigation.

### Cost

Arbitration is not necessarily less expensive than litigation. Filing a lawsuit usually costs less than arbitration fees (such as paid to the American Arbitration Association). With arbitration, you are still paying for lawyers, and perhaps experts, but also the arbitrator's fees – which, because they are usually retired lawyers or judges, are not cheap.

In a low dollar dispute, arbitration may not be practical. Your contract could provide that disputes under the small claims limit be tried in small claims court and reserve arbitration for higher dollar disputes.

The biggest cost savings usually seen in arbitration is the lack of pre-trial jockeying and motions and of extensive discovery. Discovery may or may not be entertained by the arbitrator; you can limit or prohibit discovery in the terms of the dispute resolution language in your contract.

## Confidentiality

Arbitration is not a public trial; rather it is conducted privately with only the concerned parties attending. There is no public record. Although the parties may have contractually agreed that the prevailing party may file the decision with a court of competent jurisdiction for enforcement (this is common), the contract language may otherwise provide for non-disclosure.

## Basis of Decision

In a courtroom, the judge is constrained by the law as it is reflected in statutes and prior decisions, and the trial will be governed by the rules of evidence. Arbitration is more flexible; arbitrators may consider any evidence or factors at their sole discretion. They have the ability to render decisions which they believe are equitable, which a judge bound by rules of evidence, statutes and legal precedent may be unable to reach. Unfortunately, this can cut both ways.

### Expertise

One of the strongest arguments for arbitration is the opportunity to present your case to an arbitrator who is experienced, or even expert, in construction – as opposed to a judge or jury who likely have no expert knowledge or relevant experience. But you have to assure this by requiring in your contract language that the arbitrator meet certain criteria relating to experience and expertise.

### Appeal

**224**

There is no appeal to an arbitrator's decision. You're done. The winner files the judgment with the local court of jurisdiction and you are bound by the decision, absence proof of malfeasance by the arbitrator. Errors in procedure, evidence considered (or ignored) or the like are immaterial.

The choice of litigation or arbitration is between you and the parties with whom you contract. Hopefully this overview gives you sufficient information to make an informed decision. Your best decision: pay fairly for the work you want; don't be unreasonable; work for a solution rather than point blame; have good documents; keep good records; put all changes, decisions and instructions in writing; choose reputable people to work with and treat them fairly.

## Awards

Most often arbitration awards are in the form of remedies, as opposed to cash. Therefore, your contract should have some language about how post arbitration or litigation remedy work is to be managed. It is not likely that you and your contractor will be on speaking terms after an arbitration, yet he has to return to your property, even into your home, to perform the remedy you have just been awarded. It is good to include contract language providing that any remedial work ordered by judgment be overseen by an independent third party and that the expense of that oversight be paid by the contractor (who is presumably the non-prevailing party in the matter). Further, have language directing the arbitrator to appoint the party, set the extent and limits of their oversight and authority, and their rate of pay. This interposes a neutral party between you and your builder and relieves you of having to interact with him.

225

# FINAL ACCEPTANCE

The big day has arrived – the project is completed, or so your contractor tells you. There are actually two stages of completion: substantial completion and really, really done. Substantial completion means that all the major work on the project is completed, the premises are ready for occupancy and that a final building inspection may be ordered and a Certificate of Occupancy obtained. It does not mean that there are not still some things left to do.

For instance, a building may be substantially completed but lacking a door knob to the master bedroom (because it is a special order and will not arrive for another month). This does not mean that the building cannot be occupied and used; nor does it mean that payment can be withheld from the contractor. Instead, at substantial completion the parties to the contract will walk the project and make a list of what is left to complete. These items should all be minor items; for instance, being all done except for installing carpet would not be substantial completion. A missing kitchen sink would not be substantial completion (because the building could not be used).

---

### CERTIFICATE OF OCCUPANCY

This is the document issued by the building official at the end of construction and after final inspection of the project by the building inspector. It is an official certification that the building, as built, was built in accordance with the approved plans and meets all applicable building codes. Maintain this document with the important records of your house. It can come in very handy when it comes time to sell, especially if questions are asked about the improvements you have done to your home.

---

## The Punchlist

The parties will agree to a list of items left to be completed or fixed (the "punchlist") and a date by which they are to be completed. A reasonable amount of money will be withheld from the final payment to assure their completion. (Hold more than the actual cost; usually one and a half or two times the amount.) Both parties should sign the punchlist. Once the punchlist items are completed, the contractor has fulfilled his contract obligations and all remaining monies due to him, including retainage, should be paid.

Be sure the punchlist is specific. Carefully describe the flaw to be remedied and the location. For instance: "drywall ding on west living room wall approximately 3'6" from south corner; approximately 5' above floor." Also, some items may be allowed greater or lesser amounts of time to remedy. Your contract should include general language regarding completion times for punchlist and warranty items. It should also give you the right to remedy punch or warranty items if your contractor has not done so by the deadline; and to keep the amount of money it cost you to do so as an automatic contract adjustment (change order) requiring only documentation, but not the contractor's further consent or signature. An alternative, although an awkward one and seldom used, is to assign each item on the punchlist a dollar value.

You must, however, give him reasonable notice – the punchlist, a written memo, an email, or a letter. You need to document this. Warranty work is a notorious source of disputes and litigation. Your best bet is to choose a good contractor to begin with.

## Warranty                                                   227

Your contractor does have a continuing warranty obligation after completion of the work. Specifying his warranty obligations should be included in his contract. A typical warranty is a materials and workmanship warranty usually issued for one year. Many appliances or equipment items have manufacturers' warranties which may be for a longer period of time. If your contractor purchased any of these items for you, he should assign the warranty to you in writing. He should also give you the warranty registration cards for you to fill out and return in your name.

In many states there is a longer statutory warranty period, often up to ten years for structural defects. Although many builders' contracts include exclusionary language such as "no warranty or guarantee which is not specifically set forth herein is made or implied", statutory warranties cannot be disclaimed or waived and any contract language which purports to do so will be severed from the contract.[64] Warranties do not cover normal wear and tear, failure to maintain or negligence by the buyer.

---

[64] This is the severance clause which appears in most contract boilerplate language which provides that any provision in the contract which is ruled invalid or unenforceable by a court of competent jurisdiction shall be "severed" or deleted from the contract without affecting the rest of the contract.

Your contractor should be required to collect all product brochures, owners' manuals and warranties and deliver them to you. They should be clean and pristine originals – no jobsite copies with coffee stains, tears or smears. They should be assembled in a three ring binder.

Your contractor should also deliver to you a set of as built drawings. This is a set of the original working drawings, as included in the contract, upon which he has redlined any and all deviations from the plans in the manner the project was actually built. Common deviations result, for instance, from resolving hidden conditions in remodeling work, or change orders created for whatever reason. The as builts should be a freshly printed set upon which the contractor transfers all his field notes, not the dirty, torn and worn set he used on the job. But, if that's all you can get, take it.

228

## Final Clean

A thorough final cleaning should be part of your contractor's service to you. All walls should be dusted; all cabinets, countertops, fixtures and appliances damp wiped. All tile surfaces should be cleaned of grout and dust. Glass and mirrors should be cleaned and polished. Hardwood should be damp cleaned; carpets should be vacuumed. Driveways, patios, decks and garages should be hosed down.

All fixtures should be tested.

## Moving In

An expense many homeowners overlook is the cost of moving in and out of a remodel, or into a new house. Another expense to plan for is furnishing new spaces.

But now you're in; sit down, pop a bottle of bubbly and toast yourselves. You've done it, it all worked out. Enjoy!

229

# conclusion

# IT'S YOUR PROJECT

You must take responsibility for your project. You cannot expect any other person to do that for you. Remember, every other person involved – the architect, the builder, the inspector, the workers, the superintendent – has their own interests which will always – always – be placed ahead of yours. They may coincide for a while, even for an entire project, but the underlying truth is simply a fact of life.

It is up to you to know what is going on and to be ready and able to make informed decisions. From the very beginning it is up to you to give direction to the project and to have the confidence to keep it on the track you want it on. The key is to be educated and informed; to either have the knowledge, or to know how to get it.

233

A successful project does not happen by accident; it is a collaborative effort involving many different people in many different roles. Choose your team carefully and wisely. Do not let price be your only criterion. Plan well and you will get the results you want; plan poorly and you will have problems, waste money and be unhappy. The key to good construction management is anticipation. Use the information in this book to structure your approach to your project. Anticipate what you want and how to get there.

Above all, try to enjoy the process. For me, building has always been an avocation as much as a vocation. I enjoy seeing the walls go up, the lawns planted, the picket fences and front porch swings. I savor what I build. Please, do the same.

Building is challenging, but the results can be very rewarding. Prepare for it well, fund it adequately and work with a good team and you too will enjoy building. Best of luck!

# resources

## My Favorite Building Books

*God and Mr. Gomez* by Jack Smith (a classic!)

*House* by Tracy Kidder

*Architectural Graphic Standards*

*Little Pink House* by Jeff Benedict

*Apprentice to Genius* by Edgar Tafel

## Helpful Websites

www.arcat.com — Arcat Specifications.
Website provides standard construction specifications in MasterFormat as well as manufacturers' specifications for specific products; a very robust source.

www.csinet.org — Construction Specifications Institute, publisher of MasterFormat.

www.aia.org — The American Institute of Architects, source for contract, billing and other contract documents.

| | |
|---|---|
| www.nari.org | National Association of the Remodeling Industry |
| www.uniteddesign.com | Source for residential construction building specifications |
| www.nahb.org | National Association of Homebuilders. A very robust site. |
| www.nkba.org | National Kitchen and Bath Association. |
| www.fema.gov/media/fhm/firm/ot_firm.htm | Tutorial on flood zones and maps. |
| www.iccsafe.org | International Code Council is the governing body and publisher of the International Building Code which is the most widely adopted building code in the United States. |

235

# glossary

**236**

| | |
|---|---|
| Additional Insured | A person or entity added as covered by the insurance policy of some other party. |
| Allowance | A fixed dollar amount included in a contract for the purchase of certain named items or materials, such as carpet or appliances – sometimes a fixed amount; other times an amount per unit, such as per square foot. |
| Alternate | An option to construct a portion of the project in a different way, to include or not include certain work, or to use different materials or supply different equipment. It will be stated in the bid as either an additive or a deductive dollar adjustment to the base contract. |
| As Builts | Either (a) accurate, dimensioned drawings of an existing building before the start of construction (used as the basis for planning and locating the new work); or (b) mark-ups to the approved building plans showing any deviations from the approved plans in the work as it was actually constructed. |
| Back Order | Material or parts that were not in stock when ordered; a leading cause of delay in construction. |
| Base Bid | A fixed price offered to perform a defined amount of work to which Alternates may be added or deducted. |

| | |
|---|---|
| Bid Package | The set of documents offered to contractors instructing them on how to prepare and submit a proposal to perform a defined construction project. |
| Board Foot | A measure of lumber being 1" thick by 12" wide by 1' long; to calculate board footage multiple nominal width in inches times nominal width in inches times length in feet and divide by 12; thus an 8' 2x4 would be 2x4x8/12=5.33 board feet. Lumber is priced by the thousand board feet (M/bf). |
| Bond | See Performance and Payment Bond. |
| Bozo | You know what this means; keep them off your job. |
| Building Code | The regulations adopted by the local jurisdiction governing the construction of buildings; in addition to the base building code are the electrical code, plumbing code, mechanical code and fire code. |
| Building Official | The head of the local building department; often reference is made in construction documents to the "building official"; the building official delegates his authority to the members of the building department staff, but is the ultimate arbitrator of building decisions in his jurisdiction. |
| Buy Out | What a contractor does after winning the job – he goes shopping to actually buy the materials, goods and services needed to perform the job; the goal is to "buy out" for less money than bid. |

**237**

**Certificate of Insurance** — A form used to set forth the insurance coverages of an insured. Usually addressed to a given party, but not necessarily; a certificate of insurance is normally used to create an Additional Insured endorsement.

**Change Order** — A written agreement between the owner and the contractor, or the contractor and a subcontractor, changing some aspect of the work to be included, or added or deleted from the contract; also used to change time allowed to perform.

**238**

**Code** — Short for the building code, but may also refer to the zoning code. The *International Building Code* (IBC) developed by the International Code Council has been adopted by all 50 states and the District of Columbia; the *International Residential Code* (IRC) has been adopted by 49 states and the District of Columbia; the Code Council also publishes fire, energy, plumbing and mechanical codes; more information can be found at http://www.iccsafe.org/gr/Pages/adoptions.aspx.

**Easement** — A legal right granted to someone else to use or utilize a portion of your land; common easements are for utilities such as telephone, CATV or gas located along the front or rear property lines, or for drainage.

**FAR** — Floor area ratio; the total square feet of (usually) living area divided by the total square feet of the lot; used to set a limit on the size of a building (along with height limits and set-backs).

| | |
|---|---|
| Funds Control | A method of assuring that all vendor payments are only made when earned, and that all vendors are paid in full by having a third party receive payment funds, inspect the work for completeness and approve and disburse all payments. |
| Hard Bid | A sealed competitive bid to be opened at a set date and time with the award going to the lowest qualified bidder. |
| Horizontal | Referring to construction from the surface of the earth down, including grading, utilities, drainage and roads. Compare to vertical construction. |
| HVAC | Heating, ventilation and air conditioning; usually performed by a single mechanical contractor. |
| Impact Fee | A fee levied by an authority other than the building department, such as for the local library district, fire district, parks, water, road or other public service impacted by the addition of more homes to the community; impact fees are not usually imposed on remodels of existing buildings. |
| Lay Out | Marking floors or walls with lines and notes to indicate what work is to be performed and where; often done with chalk lines and crayons; similar to Staking, but on or within a building under construction. |
| Lead Time | The time it takes to receive an item on site after it is ordered. |

**239**

| | |
|---|---|
| Lien | A legal encumbrance placed on your house by a vendor who provided services to the project to secure his alleged claim for monies owed. |
| Lien Waiver | A written statement giving up the right to place a lien. |
| Liquidated Damages | (LD's) A pre-determined, fixed monetary penalty for failure to complete a project by a certain date agreed upon between the parties; liquidated damages are used in lieu of trying to compute actual damages; it is an either/or choice. |
| Load | Weight or pressure bearing or acting upon a building element. |
| Lot Coverage | The amount of square feet of a lot covered by the first level of a building; sometimes expanded to include driveways and patios. |
| Open Book | When the contract allows the client to review his job accounting; usually in cost plus contracts when the client is required to reimburse the contractor for the actual amount spent, as opposed to a fixed fee. |
| Paper Contractor | A contractor who organizes and supervises the work but uses subcontractors to perform most or all of the actual work; often a pejorative, there is really nothing wrong with the practice. |
| Percentage Complete | The amount of either a phase or all of the work which as been completed at a point in time; the basis for making payment. |

240

| | |
|---|---|
| Plan Check | Also referred to as plans review or building department review; the review of the working drawings by the building department for compliance with the building codes. |
| Public Notice | A notice required by law or code to be published in a newspaper of general circulation; usually related to planning approvals hearings; similar would be notices to adjacent homeowners which are usually sent by certified mail. |
| Punch List | A list of items remaining to be completed or fixing. Usually prepared at the end of a job. |
| Pushing Dirt | Grading and excavation; Iron refers to the machines that do it. |
| Pull a Permit | The act of submitting plans for review by the building department and obtaining approval to build as evidenced by the issuance of a building permit. |
| R Value | A measure of the insulating value of a material, such as fiberglass insulation, or of an assembly, such as an exterior wall which included drywall, studs, insulation and siding each of which contributes to the R value. |
| Retainage | Also called retention; this is a percentage of an earned contract payment which is withheld, rather than paid, to a contractor or subcontractor; it is held as insurance against defects or omissions which might be discovered later – |

241

such as crooked framing in a bathroom that becomes apparent when the tile is being installed.

RFI — Request for information.

RME — Responsible managing employee. The person who actually hold the contractor's license for a company. Must be fully devoted to overseeing the company's construction work. Also RMO: responsible managing officer.

**242**

Rock — May be in the ground, but also refers to drywall, as in sheetrock.

Rough In — Installing electrical wires, plumbing pipes or HVAC within walls, floors or ceiling prior to drywall; plumbing rough-in also refers to installing pipes under concrete slabs prior to placement of concrete; the wires, pipes or ducts are stubbed out to receive fixtures or trims after completion of drywall and painting.

Set Back — Is the distance a building or improvement must be horizontally offset from a property line; front, rear and side setbacks typically vary.

Scale — Refers to the ratio of a plans drawing to actual size – such as $\frac{1}{4}$" = 1'0"; scale is typically referred to as quarter scale, eighth scale, etc.; architectural plans are based upon halving the inch, such as half inch, quarter inch, etc., or multiples of those subdivisions, such as 3/16; engineering plans are decimal based, dividing the inch by 10, 20, 30, 40, 50 or 60.

| | |
|---|---|
| Scope of Work | This is a written description of the work to be included in a contract or bid; for instance, a plumbing scope of work may include all the rough plumbing and setting the finish fixtures, but exclude the actual purchase and delivery of the fixtures. |
| Shop Drawing | Is a detailed drawing by a subcontractor or supplier of how an assembly will actually be built; for instance, a plan might show a wrought iron metal railing, but the actual details of the top rail and the style of the pickets is not shown; the fabricator would submit a drawing showing in detail how he plans to fabricate the parts for approval by the architect or the owner. |
| Specifications | Written standards for performing the work set forth in the plans. Together with the plans they form the construction documents. |
| Staking | Locating the position of construction on the ground starting from a survey point and taking measurements to key locations which are identified by driving wooden stakes in the ground; the stakes are often marked with different colored ribbons and written notations. |
| Stamp | Licensed architects and engineers are issued stamps by the state licensing board which they use to imprint their name and license number on a plans page or other document; doing so indicates that the page or document in question was prepared by them or under their direct supervision; after stamping the architect or engineer must sign over the stamp for the certification to be valid (see Wet Signature). |

243

**244**

| | |
|---|---|
| Submittal | Similar to a shop drawing, a submittal is detailed information about a product, say an air conditioning unit, published by the manufacturer which includes design and performance specifications; submitted to the architect or owner for approval prior to purchase. |
| Substantial Completion | When a project is essentially complete and ready for occupancy or use by the owner, but some minor items remain to be completed; for instance, the ceiling fans may be back ordered; this does not prevent the use of the building and there is no reason not to pay the contract balance less a reasonable retainage, but the contractor still must come back and install them when they arrive. |
| Take-off | Either a verb or a noun; as a verb it refers to the process of counting components in a construction projects – such as pieces of lumber – for the purpose of obtaining a cost; as a noun it is the result of performing a take-off. |
| Title 24 | Refers to the 24th part of the California Code of Regulations known as the California Building Standards Code; generally used to refer to the energy efficiency requirements for buildings; calculations must be submitted for review and approval during the permitting process. |
| Unit Price | A method of contract pricing whereby payment is made by counting units installed, such as square feet of concrete, and paying a fixed amount per unit; this type of contract is sometimes known as a variable price contract because the final amount owed is not know until the total of the units installed is added up. |

| | |
|---|---|
| Value Engineering | Is the process of reviewing the construction solutions proposed in a set of plans and proposing alternate solutions of equal quality which are less expensive; often undertaken by contractors after the award in order to reduce their costs; value engineered solutions must be approved by the architect and owner before they may be implemented; value engineering is often encouraged by owners by agreeing to approve alternatives by agreeing to share the cost savings with the contractor. |
| Variance | This is a waiver of a zoning requirement; for instance, if a portion of your building encroaches into the side yard setback, you would need to obtain a variance to allow that. |
| Vertical | Refers to the construction of buildings. Compare to horizontal. |
| Walk Through | Is an inspection of a construction project for the purposes of critiquing or accepting the work; a walk through may be preliminary or final; there may be many preliminary walk throughs during the course of a job. |
| Wet Signature | Is an original signature in ink as opposed to a photocopy; plans submitted for review must have both a wet stamp and a wet signature. |
| Wet Stamp | Similar to a wet signature, but applies to the stamp imprint. |

245

# appendix a

## MASTER FORMAT – Modified for use in residential projects

**Division 1: General Conditions**
| | |
|---|---|
| 1000 | Site Conditions |
| 1100 | Building Permit |
| 1200 | Project Management |
| 1300 | Survey/Testing/Engineering |
| 1900 | Cleanup |

**Division 2: Demolition & Site Work**
| | |
|---|---|
| 2000 | Demolition |
| 2100 | Erosion Control |
| 2200 | Earthmoving |
| 2300 | Shoring & Underpinning |
| 2500 | Site Concrete |
| 2600 | Site Utilities |

**Division 3: Concrete**
| | |
|---|---|
| 3300 | Poured in Place Foundations |
| 3400 | Concrete Slabs |
| 3500 | Decorative Flatwork |

**Division 4: Masonry & Stone**
| | |
|---|---|
| 4220 | Concrete Unit Masonry |
| 4400 | Stone Veneer |
| 4500 | Stone Floors |
| 4550 | Material Allowance |
| 4900 | Slab Granite |

**Division 5: Steel & Fabricated Metals**
| | |
|---|---|
| 5100 | Structural Steel |
| 5200 | Metal Joists |
| 5300 | Metal Decking |
| 5500 | Structural Connectors |
| 5600 | Fabricated Metals |

## Division 6:  Wood & Plastics

| | |
|---|---|
| 6100 | Rough Framing Carpentry |
| 6150 | Framing Lumber |
| 6200 | Finish Carpentry |
| 6400 | Millwork |
| 6500 | Cabinets |
| 6700 | Composites |

## Division 7:  Moisture & Thermal Protection

| | |
|---|---|
| 7100 | Foundation Waterproofing |
| 7150 | Shower Pans |
| 7200 | Thermal Insulation |
| 7270 | Firestopping & Smoke Seals |
| 7500 | Roofing |
| 7600 | Flashing & Sheetmetal |
| 7900 | Caulking & Sealants |

## Division 8:  Doors & Windows

| | |
|---|---|
| 8100 | Doors |
| 8200 | Specialty Doors & Frames |
| 8500 | Windows |
| 8600 | Skylights |
| 8700 | Hardware |
| 8800 | Glass & Glazing |
| 8900 | Louvres & Vents |

## Division 9:  Finishes

| | |
|---|---|
| 9100 | Lath & Plaster |
| 9200 | Drywall & Metal Framing |
| 9300 | Tile |
| 9600 | Flooring |
| 9900 | Painting |

## Division 10:  Specialties

| | |
|---|---|
| 10300 | Fireplaces |
| 10500 | Storage & Closet Systems |
| 10800 | Toilet & Bath Accessories |

**Division 11: Equipment**
    11400      Appliances

**Division 22: Plumbing**
    22100      Rough Plumbing
    22200      Gas Lines
    22300      Service Laterals
    22400      Finish Plumbing
    22800      Fixtures
    22850      Connect Appliances
    22900      Swimming Pools & Spas

**Division 23: Heating, Ventilation & Air Conditioning (HVAC)**
    23100      Forced Air Furnaces
    23200      Air Conditioning Units
    23300      Ducting
    23400      Fans
    23500      Controls

**Division 24: Electrical**
    26100      Underground Service
    26200      Temporary Power Service
    26300      Rough In
    26400      Low Voltage
    26500      Lighting Fixtures
    26600      Trim Out
    26650      Appliance Hook Up
    26700      Audio Visual

248

# appendix b

## STATE LICENSING REQUIREMENTS FOR RESIDENTIAL CONTRACTING

Alabama    The state of Alabama requires any general contractor working on a commercial or industrial project costing $50,000 or more to get a license. General contractors working on a residential project that costs $10,000 or more need a license.

Alaska    Alaska law requires that contractors be registered with the Department of Community and Economic Development.

Arizona    Basically, you need a license to bid on any job over $750 in Arizona.

Arkansas    To bid and work on construction projects in Arkansas that cost $20,000 or more, you must get a contractor's license.

California    With a few exceptions, all businesses or individuals who work on any building, highway, road, parking facility, railroad, excavation, or other structure in California must be licensed by the California Contractors State License Board (CSLB) if the total cost of one or more contracts on the project is $500 or more.

Colorado    General construction contractors in Colorado are not licensed by the state. You should check for license requirements at the local level. You will need a state license to do electrical or plumbing work in the state, however.

| | | |
|---|---|---|
| | Connecticut | Home improvement and new home construction contractors must be certified. Anyone working on major projects must be registered. |
| | Delaware | Contractors bidding on jobs over $50,000 must apply for a license. |
| | D.C. | Electrical, plumbing, and home improvement contractors must be licensed to work in the District Columbia of Columbia. |
| **250** | Florida | You need to be registered or certified to do construction work in Florida. You can get a "registered" contractor's license at the local level, unless a certified license is required by the county in which you want to perform the work. Contractors with a "certified" license are allowed to work anywhere in the state. |
| | Georgia | Most contractors don't need a license in Georgia. The exception is asbestos abatement and the mechanical trades. |
| | Hawaii | Hawaii requires general engineering, general building and specialty contractors to be licensed. |
| | Idaho | The state of Idaho doesn't license general contractors working on private sector residential or commercial projects. That's done at the local level. However the state does license plumbers, electricians, well drillers, fire protection sprinkler contractors, and public works contractors. |
| | Illinois | Most construction contractors don't need to be licensed in Illinois. Roofing and plumbing contractors are the exception. |

Indiana          Only plumbing contractors need to be licensed in Indiana. Public Works and Department of Transportation work must be done by certified or pre-qualified contractors. Before beginning work, you should check for license requirements at the local level.

Iowa             Plumbers and electricians must be registered with the state but are licensed at the local level. Asbestos workers, contractors and supervisors must obtain licenses for all asbestos projects.

Kansas           Kansas doesn't license construction contractors at the state level. But you should check for licensing requirements at the local level.

**251**

Kentucky         Electrical, plumbing and HVAC contractors have to be licensed in Kentucky.

Louisiana        To do construction work in Louisiana you need to be licensed by the State Licensing Board for Contractors.

Maine            General building contractors do not need a license in Maine. You'll need to be licensed to do asbestos abatement work, or electrical or plumbing contracting.

Maryland         General construction contractors don't need a license to work in Maryland. You will need a license to do electrical, plumbing or HVACR contracting, or work on home improvement projects.

Massachusetts          Anyone who supervises construction work or demolition (even a crew of one) needs a license.

| | |
|---|---|
| Michigan | Contractors working on residential or a combination of residential and commercial buildings must be licensed. Electricians, plumbers and HVAC contractors also have to be licensed. |
| Minnesota | The Minnesota Department of Commerce licenses residential builders and remodelers. |
| Mississippi | A certificate or license is required for all but the smallest construction and remodeling projects. |
| Missouri | The state of Missouri doesn't license construction contractors. |
| Montana | All construction contractors and subcontractors must register with the Department of Labor and Industry if they have employees. Those contractors without employees may register, but are not required to do so. |
| Nebraska | All contractors doing business in counties with a population of 100,000 or more need a license to do business. Nonresident contractors doing business in Nebraska must register with the Nebraska Secretary of State and the Nebraska Department of Revenue. All electricians have to be licensed. |
| Nevada | You must be licensed to bid or work on construction jobs in Nevada. |
| New Hampshire | Only certain types of specialty contractors are licensed: asbestos and lead abatement contractors, electrical contractors and plumbing contractors. |

New Jersey    You must register to be in the business of building new homes in New Jersey. You must also warrant each new home you build and provide warranty follow-up services. Plumbers and electricians are licensed in New Jersey.

New Mexico    Construction contractors must be licensed in New Mexico.

New York    Except for asbestos abatement work, all construction work in New York is regulated at the local level.

North Carolina    To work as a general contractor on projects costing more than $30,000 in North Carolina, you must get a license from the North Carolina Licensing Board for General Contractors. Electrical, plumbing, heating and fire sprinkler contractors must be licensed.

**253**

North Dakota    You must have a license in North Dakota to work on any job costing $2,000 or more.

Ohio    The state of Ohio doesn't license contractors. The municipality where work is done does that. However the Ohio Construction Industry Examining Board issues Qualification Certificates for plumbing, electrical, HVAC, hydronics, and refrigeration contractors. Landscapers need to be licensed if they plant trees or shrubs.

Oklahoma    Oklahoma doesn't license resident construction contractors, except in the electrical, mechanical and plumbing trades. But there are some special requirements for nonresident contractors.

Oregon    If you're paid for any construction activity, you need to register with the Oregon Construction Contractors Board.

Pennsylvania  Contractors are not licensed in Pennsylvania. However the Department of Transportation has certain requirements for public works contractors.

Rhode Island  If you build, repair, or remodel one- to four-family dwellings in Rhode Island, you must register with the Contractors' Registration Board. Some specialty trades must be licensed in Rhode Island.

South Carolina  To do residential building over $200 and commercial building over $5,000 in South Carolina you must be licensed.

South Dakota  South Dakota certifies or licenses only asbestos abatement, electrical and plumbing contractors.

Tennessee  You must have a license to do construction work in Tennessee.

Texas  Only specialty contractors, including HVAC, fire sprinkler systems, plumbing, and well drilling/pump installation specialists, need to be licensed in Texas.

Utah  To do construction work in Utah you need a license from the Division of Occupational and Professional Licensing. Electricians and plumbers have to be licensed.

Vermont  Contractors need to be certified to do asbestos or lead abatement and licensed to do electrical or plumbing work.

Virginia  Some construction contractors must be licensed in Virginia. Trade licenses are required for electrical, plumbing, HVAC, gas fitting, asbestos abatement and lead abatement work.

| Washington | To do construction work in Washington you must register with the Washington Department of Labor and Industries. Electricians and plumbers must be licensed. |
| --- | --- |
| West Virginia | Construction contractors have to be licensed in West Virginia. |
| Wisconsin | Most residential builders must have a state credential. Electricians, plumbers and some specialty trades must have a state credential. |
| Wyoming | All contractors, except electrical, are licensed at the local (city or county) level. However, the state requires everyone doing electrical work in Wyoming to be licensed. |

255

appendix B

# index

259

260

8699498R10153

Printed in Great Britain
by Amazon.co.uk, Ltd.,
Marston Gate.